Soccer Tough II
Advanced Psychology
Techniques for Footballers

by Dan Abrahams

BENNION
KEARNY

Published by Bennion Kearny Limited
6 Woodside
Churnet View Road
Oakamoor
B13 8BU

www.BennionKearny.com

For all those in sport striving to be
the very best they can be….

Acknowledgements

Firstly, I'd like to thank my publisher James at Bennion Kearny for all his support and advice over the past four years. I'd also like to thank my family –Mum, Dad and Zoe – for their unwavering support.

Thanks to footballers Yannick Bolasie, Kelly Smith, Rachel Yankey, Marley Watkins, and strength and conditioning coach Rayan Wilson for supporting this project and for allowing me to tell the world about their soccer mindset.

A big thanks to all those players and coaches who enjoy and support my work. I learn from you all every day and appreciate the time you take to praise and challenge my work.

Finally, the biggest thanks of all to my amazing wife Heidi, without whose unfailing support there would be no book. Thank you for being the best editor, the most helpful critic, the most enthusiastic fan, and the most caring and loving wife.

*

Rayan Wilson, strength & conditioning coach at Back2action can be contacted at rayanwilson@back2action.co.uk (www.back2action.co.uk)

About the Author

Dan Abrahams is a registered sport psychologist specialising in soccer. He works with players, coaches, clubs and soccer organisations globally and is passionate about de-mystifying sport psychology for everyone involved in the beautiful game.

His soccer tools and techniques have been used by some of the leading coaches in the game, and he has become the go-to guy for elite professional players who want to improve the mental side of their game.

As a former professional golfer, Dan holds a First Class Honours Degree in psychology and a Master's Degree in sport psychology. He is a speaker in demand at universities and colleges, and has delivered his positive, practical and upbeat messages at conferences and to governing bodies around the world.

Dan has spread his soccer psychology philosophies across the soccer globe by using social media and his mindset techniques are now used across Europe, the USA, the Middle East, the Far East and Australasia.

Follow Dan at **@DanAbrahams77**

Also follow Dan on Instagram: **danabrahamssport**

Table of Contents

Introduction

I hope you're sitting comfortably. We're going to have a conversation. We're going to have a chat about your favourite thing in the world. We're going to talk about your soccer.

This is going to be an honest discussion – I need to know plenty about your game if I'm going to be able to help you. I need to be able to see your soccer through your eyes.

So, I want you to open up to me. I want you tell me about the thoughts and feelings you experience when you train. I want you to tell me how you're preparing for an upcoming game. And I want to discuss what you're trying to achieve going into a match. Tell me in detail – the more I know about your game the greater I can impact your soccer.

By the time we're finished talking, you're going to see soccer in a completely different way. I'm probably going to bust some myths you might have about how you should train and what great pre-match preparation looks like. And I'm confident I'm going to give you some 'aha!' moments – some great answers to some of the long term challenges you've faced on the football pitch.

I must warn you, however, that this isn't always going to be a comfortable ride or an easy journey. For as long as you are working with me I need you to understand that comfort is the enemy of improvement. Perhaps the most impressive thing about champions – in all sports – is their ability to slide the scale of relaxation as they learn and compete. They know when to turn up the volume of intensity and stretch their comfort zone, but they equally know when they should slow down and loosen up. The knowledge and application of this balancing act is central to their development and their play.

Despite my tough stance on your soccer, at the heart of this book is *enjoyment*. I want you to enjoy your football. I want you to play freely and express yourself. I want you to experience the thrill of seeing yourself get better, seeing yourself become more skilful, and experience the sense of fulfilment that will accompany the small successes that follow effective learning.

A Mental Structure

Over the past decade I've noticed a consistent pattern to the challenges my soccer clients face. During that crucial first session my questions, more often than not, uncover a lack of direction in their game. They want to get better, but they don't necessarily know how to. Most players struggle to tell me what their individual development programme is. They don't always have specific training goals that will help them be the very best they can be. They go into training focused on being good but they find it difficult to define what good looks like. There is seldom a plan. There is rarely a structure to their training session.

This word – structure – is important. A common thread across the mentality of many of the soccer players I meet is the lack of a mental structure they have on a daily basis. And just as they're not as organised as they could be with their training thoughts, so they lack this mental structure *on* the pitch.

How do you prepare for a game mentally? Do you have a mental structure when you step onto the pitch? Do you have a routine on matchday that helps you find your high performance mindset? Do you know how to manage yourself from the first whistle to the last?

And what about after the match? Do you analyse your game while it's fresh in your mind so you can learn from what went well and understand what you need to work on? Do you know how to be tough on yourself and kind on yourself at the same time?

If the answer is 'no' to most of these questions then this book will provide you with some answers. This book will help you fashion a mental structure to complement the work you will be doing technically, tactically and physically.

Practice

The attitude that accompanies you when you arrive at the training pitch will heavily determine how good you get at soccer. That sounds obvious, right? Come to training with a good attitude and you'll improve. But I don't think a footballer's practice attitude is obvious at all. I think many soccer players (and many soccer coaches for that matter) define training attitude in highly simplistic terms.

A great attitude starts with an open mind – a mind that places no limits on ability. Soccer players who believe they can't certainly won't, whereas footballers who make the decision that there are no boundaries to their game will discover just how good they can be. We'll discuss the specifics of this type of mentality in chapter one.

The trajectory of your soccer is influenced by your ability to see what better looks like. A vision of the level above you, and then a plan to get there, lies at the heart of what we know, in science, about the art of improving. If you don't know what you need to develop, you'll struggle to be a great learner. You need a clear and concise plan of how you are going to work to achieve your goals. Without one you'll be directionless. Chapters two and three will introduce you to what I call the training script.

A world-class training attitude also includes an understanding of your comfort zone. To develop skill, you have to stretch this zone of comfort and for many sessions you may find you need to practice outside of this zone. Chapter four will familiarise the reader with my concept of intentional training and chapter five will present the story of how one of the greatest footballers in the women's game was able to train her brain as she trained her game.

We close this first section of the book with a message related to improving your game. Chapter six asks you to *reach and stretch*. Champion soccer players are always striving to improve by training at the edge of what they feel is possible for their game. They reach and stretch. They reach and stretch for better. They reach and stretch for improved skill. They reach and stretch for quicker, stronger and higher. It is by reaching and stretching in training, for heights beyond what you thought possible – out of comfort zones – that you will find out how good a soccer player you can be.

Prepare

The mental preparation of a soccer player is a private affair. Most have their personal rituals, and just about every footballer will physically prepare to play in some way.

When I ask footballers about their match preparation, it's usual to hear things related to nutrition and exercise. Players will eat a few hours before play and they will stretch out their muscles to ready them and to lessen the chance of injury.

But when I ask them to clarify how they prepare mentally, I am often met with silence. This lack of knowledge, related to the mental side of preparation, has to change. The modern day footballer should be as passionate about preparing his mind to play as much as his body because without the mental qualities of focus and confidence he will be unable to express his physicality. He jeopardises his technical efficiency and he may not be able to compete tactically and strategically. Section two of this book will provide the information needed to fill your mental preparation gaps.

What can be more important pre match than putting in place habits to build your confidence and energy for the game ahead? In chapter seven, I will present a concept that will enable you to identify the ingredients of confidence and the factors that affect your energy. By pinpointing the things that build your confidence and by isolating the factors that raise your energy, you can prepare to play with these important mind and body components. Leaving nothing to chance starts before kick off in the quiet depths of your mind.

Chapter eight will look at one of my most important soccer psychology tools. Every footballer, irrespective of the level they compete at, should have a match script – a set of instructions that they carry with them onto the pitch. In this chapter, I am going to tell you how to create a simple yet powerful script to help you focus your mind and centre your attention.

Once you have a match script in place, you will need to know how to execute it. You need to know how to bring your concentration back to the script when times get tough. In chapters nine and ten you will get to learn about your two controllers – the two self-management techniques you can use to stay on script. I'd like you to become world-class at using these two controllers. Soccer is a quick sport and you have to make sure you use your controllers to play at your very best every second and every minute of every match.

The final two chapters in this section provide you, the footballer, with some mental tools to try out before you go and play. Chapter 11 will teach you about one of the most popular techniques in sport psychology – visualisation. And chapter 12 covers the uncommon practice of thinking about what you'll do if it goes wrong in the heat of battle – preparing for the worst. Champions know exactly how to counteract the 'what if' moments – what if we go two goals down early? What if I make a couple of mistakes in the first five? What if I'm not feeling at my best? These 'negative' questions help the soccer player open a world of solutions. I want you thinking like that. I want you thinking like a champion.

Perform

On matchday itself, I like to insist on consistency. Reliable performers have a regular unshakeable matchday routine. They know exactly what they have to do from the minute they get up and they know precisely what they should not do.

As the match draws nearer, it's crucial to have specific tasks to complete that narrow your focus, build appropriate intensity levels, and spotlight on-pitch strategy. If you want to consistently perform highly, you need to know what your matchday routine looks like, in detail. Chapter 13 requires you to list a set of procedures that will focus your mindset.

And when you're mentally warmed up, so the moment of truth arrives. Kick off! The preparation is complete. It's you, the ball, your team mates and the opposition. Now it's showtime.

As you play, you get the opportunity to use the tools and techniques that you learnt in the preparation section. Most importantly, you get to use them to overcome negative thoughts or *squash the ANTs*. ANTs stands for Automatic Negative Thoughts and I'm going to develop the interventions I introduced to you in my first Soccer Tough book. Let's get speedy at squashing those most destructive of thoughts – the ones that tighten your muscles and slow your body down! Chapter 14 will show you how.

In Chapter 15, I get to introduce you to a great squasher of ANTs. He's a well known footballer who I've had the pleasure of working with over the last few seasons. He's a fantastic player and an even better person. Along our journey together, we've constructed a match script that suits his eyes, suits his ears, and suits his body. He'll show us how he puts it all together wrapped in a bubble of fun, freedom and focus.

Of course, playing with fun, competing with freedom, and allowing your mind to focus isn't possible if you 'think' too much on the pitch. The mind must be clear for you to play without fear. I ask all my players to strike a balance between doing and thinking – there is a mental sweet spot that all footballers can settle into. The 80/20 rule I describe in chapter 16 will help you flex your thinking muscles at the right moment and relax your thoughts at other times.

On-pitch mental techniques wouldn't be complete, of course, without lessons from the mentally toughest footballers on the planet. That accolade, I feel, lies safely with the German international team. To date they have never lost a penalty shoot-out. They even have a word in the German language to describe their fearless nature which they apply time and time again from the terrifying 12-yard spot. Chapter 17 will help you become fluent in the Germanic version of mental toughness.

Progress

Our final section is as important as the others. If you want to improve, you have to believe you can get better. You have to see yourself capable of delivering at a higher level.

The development of skill is mediated by your soccer image – the picture you house in your mind of yourself as a footballer. Your ability to play well, in each and every game, also depends on this internal image. It's a powerful indicator of what you can achieve in soccer today and tomorrow.

Chapter 18 will give you a tool to measure your soccer image. Do you see yourself in a positive or negative light? Is your soccer image healthy enough to allow you to develop your game?

Building your soccer image starts with knowing where you are now. The footballer who thinks and acts a level above has, in my opinion, an optimistic view of herself. By thinking big, she can build the developmental scaffolding that her game needs to get better.

Chapter 19 offers specific game analysis patterns to grow your soccer image and progress your game. Do you know how to analyse your performances to maintain confidence? Maybe you do. But do you know how to analyse the weak parts of your game whilst expanding your self-belief? This chapter teaches you to improve your soccer image whilst being tough on yourself and your performance.

Of course, your performances won't be stellar if you're not physically fit and your body isn't strong and in balance. It's difficult to be mentally tough in your soccer when your body is weak. Just as mind affects body, so body impacts mindset. Chapter 20 introduces you to one of the world's most innovative football-specific strength and conditioning coaches. This trainer is becoming the go-to guy for players at the top level of the game in England and his work on their soccer physiques stretches further than their bodies. As he works their physicality, he fine-tunes their mind.

The final two chapters provide, I hope, some inspiration. They will give you a guide to thinking your way towards an improved soccer image as well as a number of tools to retain a positive image through tough times and periods when it feels like you're not going to get better.

Passion with Precision

I'm passionate about helping soccer players of all levels and ages get better and the strategies in this book are designed for everyone in mind.

I've written it for you, the soccer player. The hungry, craving-for-better soccer player. The structure in this book is designed to help the best in the world as well as the Sunday league player. Anyone who wants to improve can benefit from it. You can take the techniques onto the five-a-side pitch with you, or you can use them in the stadium in front of 50,000 screaming fans.

I like to combine passion with precision. What is written on the pages of this book demands a brain that not only loves the beautiful game but which is prepared to study it with intricate detail. Champions are passionate and champions are precise.

What does better look like?

What does better feel like?

Before you turn the page, be precise with your definition of better. I'm going to show you how you can make that a reality. I'm going to show you a world of better soccer.

Practice – Introduction

People will tell you that you can't. People will tell you that it's impossible. People will tell you not to try. People will tell you not to bother.

Ignore them…

Because nobody knows just how good you can become. *Keep* going!

It is for *you* and you *alone* to determine how good you can be.

If people tell you that you are great. If people tell you that you have promise and potential. If people tell you that all you have to do is turn up. If people tell you that success is inevitable.

Ignore them…

Because nobody knows just how good you can become. *Never* get complacent!

It is for *you* and you *alone* to determine how good a soccer player you can be.

To get where you want to go, you've got to be willing to go deep with your practice. You've got to be willing to do things smarter, with greater focus and with more intention than the crowd of players around you. You've got to be willing to be a student of *your* game and a student of *the* game.

You won't become the kind of soccer player you want to be if you just think about it. That doesn't work – that's pop psychology! You have to know *how* to get the most from yourself. You have to know about effective practice protocols. Then you have to do it – you have to go practice your game with the mindset of a champion, and with the look of a winner.

I call it practice, rather than training, because the word relates better to the demands of improving skill. Training is physical, practice is mental – it's repetition, it's reinforcement, it's focus, it's intelligence, and it's comfort zone busting. It's also technical and tactical – it's new moves, it's different positioning, it's mastery, it's body control, and it's the application of new knowledge.

By the end of this section you will have a *different* practice mindset. A *better* practice mindset.

- You will know *exactly* what you need to do to get better
- You will know how to practice *effectively*
- You will know how your brain reacts and responds to practice, and you will know how to get the *most* out of this powerful 'muscle'
- You will know how to *stretch* yourself in training sessions… and how to *keep* stretching yourself

But before we get into the intricacies of world-class practice and training I'm going to help you expand your definition of talent. If you want to be the very best footballer you can be, you've got to believe in yourself – this means you've got to identify the talent you *already* possess. Everyone has talent. Everyone can be good at this game. Everyone can excel. Turn to chapter one to find out more…

1

You Have The Talent...

I have a new rule number one for you.

It isn't about positioning or movement or hold-up play or passing with progression. It isn't about strength or stamina or agility or speed. It is more impactful than any of those. It can't be seen and it can't be touched. It is personal to you but it is a non-negotiable for every soccer player around the world. And within its philosophy lies more fun, and greater levels of success.

So what is this number one rule that I want you to embrace? It's brief, it's powerful, and it will impact your game:

You have to train, you have to play, and you have to think like there are no limits to your ability.

Let me say this again – I want you to read it and digest it. I want it to become the heartbeat of your development as a footballer.

You have to train, you have to play, and you have to think like there are no limits to your ability.

Take a few minutes to imagine a footballing world where this philosophy exists for you. Imagine a mentality that sets no limits and a game that has no boundaries. Blow this up in your mind. What do you experience? What do you see? How do you feel? What are you saying to yourself? What are others saying to you? How do you hold yourself on the training pitch? What is your attitude on match day?

I say this, and I ask these questions, because I know that many footballers hold themselves back by how they see themselves as a player. They make premature judgements on how good they can become. They aren't no-limit soccer players. They don't think they have the capability to get to the next level, and then the level after that. They choose to say 'This is who I am' rather than exercise their imagination by saying 'This is who I can become'.

As a consequence, many footballers fall foul of the mental side of the game. They set their ambitions and aspirations too low. They give up too easily. They give in to the kind of destructive emotions that hold their game back – emotions such as frustration, despondency and anxiety.

If they have a bad game they walk off the pitch reinforcing the notion that they can't, they won't, and they never have. Their negative brain beats them up and enforces a zone of comfort around the average. *"I knew it was unrealistic to think I could have a good game against this kind of opposition. I know where I really belong, and it's not at this level!"*

A footballer who trains and plays with self-limiting beliefs will never truly discover how good she can be. If she practices her game with fear or intimidation, or tinged with a lack of confidence, she won't build the skill her body is capable of. If she runs onto the practice pitch overly concerned by what others think of her or preoccupied with mistakes and errors, her brain won't have the capacity to focus and subsequently learn from her coaches.

Similarly, a soccer player who thinks he can't, definitely won't. If his thoughts about his game project pictures of miscontrol and an inability to find space or retain the ball, then his inner map will become his outer reality.

And all of these negatives start with the perception you have of your talent. Your natural ability. Your inborn promise. So let me repeat:

You have to train, you have to play, and you have to think like there are no limits to your ability.

Talent in Abundance

I think you have talent in abundance. I can say this confidently because I know, from the very fact that you are reading these pages, that you already have one form of talent for soccer – passion. If you didn't love the game you wouldn't be taking the time to read my words.

Having a passion for something is a talent. It may not be physical in its quality. It may not trap a ball or ghost you past a defender but let me be clear – you can't be any good at something if you don't have a passion for it. Passion is the running start that edges you into the lead!

There are many who are involved in soccer – coaches, volunteers, parents – who see talent in a one-dimensional way. When they hear the words 'natural ability' they conjure up an inner movie of a young player dribbling through the opposition and bulging the back of the net with an unstoppable shot into the top right corner of the goal. They picture big and tall and strong. They think of effortless footballing wizardry made from a cocktail of quick feet and impossible vision.

I don't deny the existence of physical talent. That would be like denying the existence of the sun and the moon and the sky. There is no doubt that some find it easier to play soccer than others. They may have an extraordinary physical presence through height, strength and speed. Or they may have a way with the ball that, at first glance, appears unteachable. They bring the ball down effortlessly, they consistently spot the killer pass and they strike the ball perfectly every time.

These are physical talents and they are important. But their impact eventually lessens without another form of talent – the talent I think is most important. Mindset talent.

Mindset talent is what lies inside you, hidden from view, away from the prying eyes of scouts, teammates, parents, coaches and volunteers. It is my belief that in football, the internal drives the external. Soccer success is as much about your inner qualities as it is about your outer capabilities, because the outside (your skill) is heavily influenced by the inside (your mindset).

If developing a soccer game is like building a house, then mindset talent is the mortar to the bricks of physical talent. Without mortar, the house will topple over. Without mindset talent, physical talent won't help you fulfil your potential. You will only go so far!

And the exciting thing is that there are countless mindset talents that you may possess. Determination is a talent. As is dedication. Patience is a talent. So is focus. In fact, we can split focus into several talent categories:

- The ability to focus on the pitch under pressure
- The ability to focus following distraction
- The ability to focus on doing the right things every day to be the best you can be

Having travelled the footballing globe I've learnt that we have all become a little too obsessed with what we see on the outside. We don't appreciate the skills that are inherent on the inside. Skills like confidence, focus, self-belief, discipline, listening, dedication, learning and understanding. Skills like emotional management, effort, perseverance, self-regulation, self-awareness, thinking flexibility and leadership. Skills like the ability to cope through tough times, self-sufficiency, motivation, empathy, initiative, self-assessment and the ability to get on with others.

These are abilities and talents too. They make or break players, depending on their presence or absence. They influence the level a soccer player competes at, and how quickly a player gets there. They also mediate the length of a career and the enjoyment that grows from playing competitively.

A footballer wins with his mind as much as his feet.

Soccer Mindset

Soccer is as much a game of mindset and mentality as it is a physical discipline because of its complexity. It's not a sport where you are rejected or retained because of what your genes have given you.

There is far more chance of you being ruled out of becoming a world class athlete than there is of you failing to become a world class footballer. Science tells us that you've probably got to have a lot of fast twitch muscle fibres to win a 100-metre race. Likewise, you've probably got to be over six feet tall to compete internationally in the high jump. In contrast, you have to be small and weigh very little to be a jockey riding winners at the Kentucky Derby, the Grand National or the Melbourne Cup.

Similarly, it's unlikely that you'll compete in the NBA if you're five feet five inches in height. You've got no chance of winning the heavyweight championship of the world if you're naturally a middleweight. And it's almost impossible for a male tennis player to compete successfully on the ATP Tour if he is under five feet five inches tall.

Soccer has no such restrictions. Arguably, the two best players in the world, at the time of writing, are Lionel Messi and Ronaldo. Two men with completely contrasting body shapes. One, a physical specimen, the other lacking height and strength. But both at the pinnacle of the sport.

Being small never ruled out Messi or Xavi Hernandez or Iniesta. Growing up at La Masia, the Barcelona Academy, they could have weaved a different internal story. They could have told themselves that they weren't big enough to play top-level football. They could have given into thoughts that restricted their progression.

But they didn't. They believed in the abilities they had – both their physical and their mindset abilities. And with the help of their coaching staff they set about becoming the very best they could be. They dug away at the bottomless pit that is human potential.

Are you digging away at your bottomless pit? Do you see yourself as a no-limit footballer?

Soccer is a game of thinking. It's a game of awareness, anticipation and decision-making. It's a game of speed of thought. It's a game of intelligence – of tactical understanding and of pattern recognition. It's a game that requires knowing what to do at the right time – with confidence. It's a complex game, impossible to master.

The physically gifted aren't granted an exclusive licence to make great decisions. The physically talented aren't the only ones who can learn to play intelligently. Everyone can improve these types of skills. So, everyone has a bottomless pit of potential.

You have to train, you have to play, and you have to think like there are no limits to your ability.

No-One Really Knows

No-one really knows just how good you can be. Everyone is guessing. No-one knows how much you can improve your skills. No-one really knows where your final destination in soccer is.

I want you to see your potential as limitless. You have talent in abundance. You have the ability to be the best you can be, and no-one can tell you just how good that is.

You have to train, you have to play, and you have to think like there are no limits to your ability.

There were plenty who said David Beckham wouldn't make an impact at Real Madrid. But he did! Did current Manchester United defender Chris Smalling give up on his dreams when he played non-league football in England? Of course he didn't! And his persistence paid off – he won a move to one of the biggest clubs in the world.

I have worked with, and continue to work with, players who play one, two and, sometimes, even three divisions below what they are capable of. I strive to help them train and play with no limits. I firmly believe a footballer who spends time thinking about playing football outside perceived limitations will break down self-imposed barriers... fast! I want that for you; in fact, you need to personally insist on it for yourself!

Your Talent, Your Decision

The dreams you have for your game, and the goals you set yourself, are for you – and you alone – to decide. Never let anyone tell you what you can and cannot achieve in soccer.

You have to train, you have to play, and you have to think like there are no limits to your ability.

Nothing and no-one can hold you back. Nothing and no-one can tell you what you can and cannot achieve on the pitch. It is for *you* to decide how good you can be. It is for *you* to decide the limits of your capability. It is for *you* to decide your future in soccer.

Technique Number 1

You have to train, you have to play, and you have to think like there are no limits to your ability.

2

Profile the Next Level

The champions, the great ones, have something in common.

Usain Bolt, Miguel Cabrera, Serena Williams, Sir Bradley Wiggins, Inbee Park, Michael Phelps, Rory McIlroy, LeBron James – they all have something in common.

Missy Franklin, Ronaldo, figure skater Mao Asada, snowboarder Kelly Clark, Tim Tebow, Homare Sawa, David Beckham – they all have something in common.

They may play different sports, they may demonstrate different skills, they may display different body shapes, they may be from different continents, and they may compete on different sides of the world – but they all have something in common.

To become a champion and to remain at the highest of sporting heights they have had to spend time profiling the next level. During their career they have examined, in intricate detail, what 'better' looks like and what 'better' feels like.

And that is what champions do. Champions are restless. They yearn for more. They have an itch for improvement – one that is never completely soothed. And they don't say "*This is who I am*". They say "*This is who I can become*". They are passionate about 'better'. The flame of excellence burns strongly in their feet, through their bodies and across their minds.

To be the very best *you* can be, to explore your bottomless pit of potential, you must do what a champion does. You, yourself, must profile the next level. You must take a cold, hard look at your game, you must become acquainted with what 'better' looks like, and you must set your path of improvement towards being the kind of player you want to be.

To be the best you can be you have to profile the next level.

Becoming the Best

Becoming the best that you can be isn't limited to physical effort and sweat. It's not just about demonstrating the kind of exertion that speeds your heart rate. And it shouldn't reduce you to running around like a headless chicken.

This is where many soccer players get confused. They think because they train with intensity, they will improve. They think that scoring a couple of goals in practice equals a successful session. They believe that being the 'best trainer' is enough. Wrong, wrong and wrong!

Intensity and effort obviously do count, but they should only be a *part* of your training armoury. Scoring goals and keeping clean sheets are the outcomes you want on matchday but are not the critical essentials on the practice pitch. And being nominated as best trainer doesn't automatically invite you to the table of champions. Practice excellence is far more subtle and requires far more intelligence. That is why improvement in soccer can be so elusive.

Becoming the best you can be requires you to take ownership of your game. It is not up to anyone else to make you better. *You* are accountable. It is for *you* to set your practice targets. It is for *you* to break down your game and formulate a strategy to improve.

To be the best you can be you have to profile the next level.

Unfortunately, all too often, I see the reverse. I meet players who rely on others to set the pace. They want to be told what to do. They depend on the coaching staff. These players may well be fit and strong and skilful, but they aren't students of *the* game and they aren't students of *their* game. They don't progress with the kind of rapidity and speed that a champion demands of himself or herself. It is up to the individual soccer player to take responsibility for his or her learning and his or her improvement.

Becoming the best you can be also requires intelligence. It requires self-awareness and game understanding. It involves a microscopic look at your current abilities with openness and honesty. You need to know what you need to get better at, and you need to know what 'better' looks like. To do this you have to exercise your imagination – you have to imagine a game that is superior to yours. You need to project an inner movie of the moves and the plays you want for your footballing future. This will act as an exciting turbo-charged template for you to work towards – relentlessly and ruthlessly.

To be the best you can be you have to profile the next level.

The Breakdown

Let's take a look at the footballing components that make up your game. We have five in total –

1. Technical
2. Tactical
3. Physical
4. Psychological
5. Social

I'd like you to start making a list of the areas you believe you need to improve in your game. If you don't want to write them down, that's fine – just keep a mental note.

As you start to create your list you need to make sure you are considering:

- Strengths (that need maintaining and developing)
- Weaknesses (that need improving)
- The responsibilities within your role on the pitch
- What better players (perhaps the world's best) do, and how they do it

Strengths shouldn't be ignored – they will stop being assets if you overlook them. Players need a weapon to show off and to weather the storm of a bad game. Strengths help you express your game confidently and can make you look good in a mere minute – even if the other eighty-nine minutes have been filled with mistakes.

It's not negative to spend some time thinking about your weaknesses – it's constructive. How can you be the best player you can possibly be if you don't know what's holding you back or keeping you at the same level? Awareness of your weaknesses is your first step in turning them into strengths.

Paying close attention to the responsibilities in your role is crucial in this process because different roles on the soccer pitch have distinct physical and technical demands. Use this activity as an opportunity to really think about the specific challenges in your position – the requirements when working forward and working back defensively. If you cover several positions, then take the time to consider all the roles you play, or have played, on the pitch.

Finally, it is useful to consider the games of other players who compete in your position. You may choose to reflect upon the football of a clubmate who plays in the team above you. Meditating on the game of players who are only a little bit better than you can be a really effective way of deciding what you need to get better at. Alternatively, you might choose to picture the game of a footballer competing at the elite level – thinking about what they do on and off the ball provides tough-to-reach markers that can inspire you to improve your skills.

The Nitty-Gritty

Strengths, weaknesses, your role and the responsibilities within that role, as well as the game of others. You now need to take the time to think about these aspects with relation to the five components of the game – technical, tactical, physical, psychological and social.

Technical

Firstly, you may wish to think about the technical component of the game. A few examples here include first touch, shooting, passing, dribbling and crossing. How well do you trap and control a ball? What is your passing and shooting technique like? Do you get clean strikes most of the time? Do you get enough power behind your shots, and are your passes accurate? If they are average, can they be good? If they are good, can they be great?

What is your technique like, when compared to those who are the best in the world? What do they do better than you? How do you think they do it? What would you like to work on that could nudge you ever so slightly closer to their game?

As you take a little time to create an impression of the technical side of your game in your mind, give yourself a mark out of 10 (or out of 100 if you'd prefer) for each of the areas you hone in on. Make top marks – a 10/10 or 100/100 world class. Where are you on this scale? Do this slowly and deliberately – excellence requires an acute sense of self-awareness and game awareness.

Tactical

When you've finished analysing your technique, move on to the tactical side of the game – positioning, awareness, movement, shape, your knowledge of formation, and set pieces. Do you know what your coach wants from a tactical point of view? Do you know when to go forward and when to stay back? Do you know how to see more and do you know where to go and where to be at the right time?

Once again, get a vivid impression of a world-class player who competes in your position in your mind. What is he or she doing that is better tactically? Do they see more? Do they do it quicker? How can you see more and do more at greater speed?

The tactical and the technical sides of the game gel together to determine the quality of your skill execution and your ability to make effective split-second decisions. Poor technique influences the capacity to which you can execute the tactical side of the game – consistent poor first touches lead, not only to a loss of possession, but to a slower game. With poor technique the picture around you changes – good positions adopted by your teammates become hard-to-complete passes. In contrast, a great first touch will give you an extra second to make the right decision – do I keep hold of the ball or do I release it? A crisp, accurate pass allows your team to keep hold of possession and gives you time to find the right attacking position and progress up the pitch.

What needs to go better technically? What do you need to improve tactically?

I need a better first touch and an improved body shape when receiving the ball – to have time to make better decisions.

I need more accurate shots to help me score more.

I need to become more aware of what's going on around me – to see the positions of teammates and the opposition quicker – I need to check my shoulders more.

Physical

Now you've completed your technical and tactical self-analysis, take some time to think about what you need to enhance physically?

Do you need to be more powerful in the air or stronger in the tackle? Do you need to increase your range of motion or your flexibility for injury prevention? Are you quick enough? Can you develop a kick of speed to be first to the ball more often? Do you last the distance or do you find your energy levels waning in the early stages of the final quarter hour, well before the final whistle is blown?

With greater physicality comes better technique. With improved technique comes superior tactical execution.

Isn't that domino effect exciting – one component of the game feeds positively into another! A chain reaction of excellence that is compulsive and addictive and fun and powerful in equal measures.

- *I need to work on my fast feet to help me get around the pitch better – I need to work on my agility*
- *I need to be stronger in the tackle – I need to work on my upper body strength*
- *I need to have more energy after I make an explosive run deep into the opposition's half – I need to work on my recovery after intense runs*

Psychological and Social

You now know what 'better' looks like in three components. Let's explore the fourth and fifth. I want you to consider the mental and social parts of your game – use the words we've already uncovered in this book. Game transforming words such as focus, confidence, belief, intensity, emotion, listening, learning, discipline and commitment.

How do you see yourself as a soccer player? Does the image you house of yourself, in your mind, relate to the reality of your game? Are you actually a lot better than you think you are? Do you lack that bit of belief in your game? This mental picture contained in your mind – that relates to your football – is something I call your soccer image. It's an important area of your psychology that I will address in section four.

What about your emotional management? Do you tend to get stressed in the lead-up to a match? If things aren't working out on the pitch do you lose your temper, or veer into hopelessness?

Soccer is a game of mindset. It's critical that you take the time to break down this area of the game and give yourself an honest appraisal.

Finally, let's think about the social side of the game. Are you always on time (or early) for training? Are you a great teammate – a strong communicator, a keen listener, an ear lender, and a strong leader or focussed follower? Are you coachable or do you have a tendency to be closed-minded?

The social side of the game is often ignored by players. Most don't see leadership as a set of behaviours with skills that need to be (and can be) developed. Many team captains enjoy displaying the black band of leadership on their arm without really exploring what it takes to be a strong leader.

Soccer players can also underestimate how important it is to help others in their team and in their squad. Assisting clubmates on and off the pitch gets to the heart of being a great teammate. Understanding the personalities and characteristics of others can help you yourself improve, can help your team win matches, and can help your club grow and prosper.

- *I need to communicate more positively when my teammates make a mistake (I tend to berate them)*
- *I need to talk to myself better when I play, especially when I make mistakes – this will help me sustain my energy and confidence*
- *I need to practice my focus during training – this will help me focus better during games*

Think About It

Take your time. Try to pick 2-5 areas under each component to focus on. Stretch yourself and think about the game outside of your comfort zone. Be detailed. That vision of better will shape your future football.

Beg, steal and borrow from others. What does your coach think? How about your parents or team mates? What about a former coach or mentor of influence. The view others have of your game is likely to be quite different from your own and that's okay. That's useful.

Once complete you'll have a list of your soccer 2.0. Perhaps a quicker, stronger game. Maybe a more skilled, more controlled game. Whatever better looks like for you, our next job is narrow down your chosen areas to develop what I call your training script.

Technique Number 2

To be the best you can be, you have to profile the next level.

3

Your Training Script

The improvement process is very similar to the kind of procedure you experience when you go to a doctor if you're not feeling well. When you visit a medical expert, they first examine you and then they provide you with a prescription.

World-class training begins with the profile you have developed in the previous chapter – this is your examination. You now have to work on your game prescription.

It is impossible to focus on developing every area you have chosen under each of your components, so I'd like you to start narrowing down your list. When I work with a client, this process is simple. After we have 'profiled the next level' I ask him or her to pick the three most urgent areas of development, the three that need to get better straight away. I want you to do the same right now.

Pick three that you'd like to focus on over the next month of training sessions. If you'd prefer to pick two areas that are weak and one area that you deem to be strong (that you'd like to maintain and magnify) then that, too, is fine.

These three 'plays' make up your training script. Your script is, as the name suggests, your prescription. In the previous chapter, you gave your game a thorough self-examination. Now you're self-prescribing. Designing a training script is a treatment champions embark on every month.

Design your training script and take small steps every month to build the game of your dreams.

It's no more complicated than that. I tend to work with footballers on a monthly basis – so, a player picks three areas to develop and maintain for a month; then, after this period of time, we review and look to change things where appropriate.

Make sure you can measure your improvement programme. You've already given yourself a mark out of 10 or out of 100 for each area – set yourself a target mark. Sure, this is quite a subjective process, but just as you've already sought advice about the next level from those who know your game best, so you can get others involved in the development of your training script. Tell a coach, a teammate or a parent what you're trying to improve. Ask them to rate you and ask them if they can monitor your script.

To help you get this process clear in your mind, I will introduce you to several training scripts that I have developed with clients over the past couple of seasons.

Premiership Goalkeeper

A few years ago, I got a phone call from a fairly well-known goalkeeper who played for a Premiership club. He told me that he was pleased with how he had been playing in his first few seasons in the face of the intense fan and media scrutiny he had experienced. And he was delighted with the way he had handled the pressure of competing in one of the world's toughest leagues.

But despite his consistent form, he was concerned. He felt his game was at a slight standstill – he wanted to get better, quicker! He wanted to cement his position at his club and compete in the World Cup for his international team. He wanted to be the very best he could be.

When I receive this kind of phone call I am always excited – a player who is passionate about excellence is a player who instantly gains my complete respect.

As I often find myself doing, I explained to him that whilst I was confident I could help him, I wanted him to understand that the work we would embark on would be gradual and subtle. I wanted him to appreciate that the improvement process sport psychology delivers can be naked to the eye – a small shift here, a tiny nudge there. It doesn't deliver big leaps in skill – just a number of small increases that adds up over time.

He accepted this. He knew that improvement wouldn't come easy. He knew that upgrading his game would take focus and trust and patience. And after a brainstorming session, in which we profiled his next level, we came up with a simple training script. It looked like this:

What? Set Position – get set quicker. Currently 5/10 (too slow and lethargic). In the next month increase this to 6/10.
How? Ask goalkeeping coach to do more practical drills that emphasise speed of set position and ask coach to be tough on him with this part of his game.

What? Catching – time jumps better on crossing ball. Currently 6/10 (inconsistent – sometimes too late or too early). Wants to increase this to 7/10 this month.
How? Take time after every training session to do more catching from crossing balls. When possible, get a teammate involved to act as a distractor and put pressure on him physically.

What? Confidence and emotional management – often feels down following a mistake. Currently 3/10 (feels very down and flat). Wants to improve this to 6/10 this month (urgent!).
How? Aim to portray confident body language after a mistake – stand tall, get on toes and be vocal with defenders (to put the mistake behind him and restore feelings of confidence).

This is a training script centred on technique, physicality and mindset. It helped this goalkeeper take greater ownership of his training. It helped him throw away that feeling of sameness and stagnation that footballers can experience in their playing careers, and drive and fight for a better standard of soccer.

A Young Defender

Last season I worked with a young English defender who played in the Women's Super League.

This promising player is a centre-back who took the time to chat with me about the challenges she felt by playing at a big club and the burden of expectation she felt every week she set foot on the pitch.

One of the ways I helped her manage the hope others had for her (amongst quite a few other psychology techniques and performance philosophies) was to build a training script. We used it as a way to channel her focus into something positive. I constantly reinforced the notion of development, improvement and learning. Ignore others – learn! Shift away from the pressure – learn! Create the game you dream of – learn!

I explained to her the importance of profiling the next level and detailed the impact a training script could have on her game. I wanted her to relax about her future – in part, by helping her plan a process to get better.

Here is a training script from one of the months we worked together:

What? *Awareness – needs to improve awareness of movement around her. Currently 4/10 (from video analysis, looks around about 5 times a minute). Wants to improve this to 6/10 this month (looking around 8 times a minute).*
How? *Do this in training – get one of the coaches to observe and remind when possible.*

What? *Be a better defender at corners – become more certain and confident. Currently 7/10 (uncertain about tactics and player roles). Wants to get to 9/10 in a month.*
How? *Talk with coaches about confusion related to tactical knowledge from set pieces (What do they want me to do?). Discuss with goalkeeper what she is thinking and looking to do when defending corners. Emphasise positive self-talk when the ball goes out of play for a corner, or when a free kick is conceded deep in the team's half.*

What? *Vocals – as a centre-back become more of a leader. Currently 4/10 (quiet, little impact with voice). Wants to get to 6/10.*
How? *Become better acquainted with speaking in and around the club more. During training, focus on being brave enough to let her voice be heard. Deal with negative thoughts related to being vocal (accept*

introversion off the pitch, but strive to be more extraverted on the pitch).

This was a first-class training script dealing with tactics, technique and mentality. As a young player, she needed help from the expert coaches she had around her. She needed to communicate and cooperate with them to a greater degree to learn about her position more quickly and effectively.

She also recognised that she needed to come out of her shell a little bit. I explained to her that it was okay to be quieter off the pitch, but her coaches wanted her to learn to be a bit more vocal under pressure. They wanted her to be able to help her teammates out when the momentum was against them – to be able to communicate confidently in relation to parts of the pitch and parts of play they couldn't see.

An Ageing Midfielder

Age is irrelevant. It's just a number. It's not a physical signature. You are never too young and you are never too old – you can always get better.

This is a message I wanted to get through to a French soccer player who competed in the lower divisions in France. He was starting to feel the effects of a long career; he was tired and slightly burnt out. But he also felt he had a couple more seasons in him and he didn't want to quit.

In order to freshen things up, as well as give him the best opportunity to remain in the first team, we worked on a training script. This is what it looked like:

What? Set piece specialist – get back to being the set piece specialist of the team by working on ball delivery and direct free kicks from just outside the area (make himself invaluable!). Currently 7/10 (inconsistent flight, not enough goals). Wants to be 9/10.
How? Work after training, flight 30 balls into the area and 30 balls into the net every day.

What? Pace – maintain pace even though getting older. Currently 6/10. Maintain at 6/10.

How? Work with a sprint coach that helps footballers gain speed.

What? Be better prepared than ever for games. Currently 8/10 (good, but could include mental skills to help get into the correct mindset more consistently).

How? Add mental rehearsal and visualisation to daily training methods. Use this to 'know' the specific challenges opponents bring to the pitch.

It was another two years before this midfielder retired. In the two seasons we worked together, he disciplined himself to updating his training script every month. His dead-ball delivery started to improve and he kept his pace. We worked tirelessly on his mindset to make sure that he kept his mental sharpness and his visual acuity. He took it seriously. Even though I joined his footballing journey when he was 34, he still had a passion to play. He still had a passion to compete. And, with practice, he found he still had the power to improve – and he did.

You Have the Power…

You have the power to improve. You have it within you to develop a game that may not have seemed possible before you started this book.

You have the power to break down football into its main components, then further split these components into specific areas that you want to build upon or improve on.

You can do this in several ways, and I advise you to begin at the beginning. You can talk with your coaches about your game. You can talk with teammates who play with you and friends who watch you. You can borrow from other, more advanced, more consistent players or you can exercise your imagination to daydream what your own personal 'better' may look like next month or next season.

Once you've profiled the next level, and compiled the evidence, you can build your training script. Champions narrow down their focus – they know they can't work on everything at once. Be intelligent and patient. Three steps forward a month will lead to an exciting future in soccer (no matter what level you aspire to).

Be clear about the importance of profiling the next level and designing a training script. The quality and efficiency of your training is the biggest determinant of your progress in soccer. The next chapter will explain why.

Technique Number 3

Design your training script and take small steps every month to build the game of your dreams.

4

Intentional Training

Greatness isn't achieved under the lights in the arena. It's not achieved in a stadium packed with passionate supporters. It's not achieved in the quarters or the semis or, indeed, the final. And it's not achieved when the ball bulges the back of the net, or when a hand tips the penalty kick around the post.

Greatness is a private affair. It's achieved behind closed doors, away from the public gaze, on the relative quiet of the training pitch.

It's achieved by repeating Rondo. It's achieved with keep-ball. It's achieved through drill and reinforcement. It's achieved during small-sided games. It's achieved while working on shape and pattern.

Greatness is built, not on match day, but during your practice sessions. I believe this with all my heart, because I believe in the power of effective and efficient practice. I believe everyone can get better. We all have a bottomless pit of potential and I believe you can dig a pit that becomes deeper and deeper with world-class training.

Just how good you can get at football, nobody knows. But what *is* known is that the quality of your training is a big determinant of your trajectory in this game. In fact, I believe that the quality and efficiency of your training is the *biggest* determinant of your progress in soccer.

The quality and efficiency of your training is the biggest determinant of your progress in soccer.

You have already taken big steps towards implementing game improvement. You have profiled the next level and you have designed a training script. You are halfway there. You now have to start putting your script into practice – and this isn't easy.

Most soccer players *want* to improve. They have a passion to get better and they train at an intensity that matches their motivation. They train with a will for progress. But *wanting* to get better and knowing *how* to get better are two different things. Most players want to and try to – but very few know *how* to.

Indeed, improving your game is challenging, it's difficult. Over the decade and a half that I've been working with footballers, I rarely find players who train with the kind of efficiency that will help them get the very most from their talent. The type that will help them be the best they can be.

So many players get stuck at the same level. They find it difficult to upgrade their game. Exploring your bottomless pit of potential by getting the very most out of your training script will take greater effort, more energy and an added focus that you probably weren't exercising yesterday. Today and tomorrow must be different! Your future training sessions must be better.

And if you want to be the very best you can be, you too need to believe in the power of practice. You too need to trust that your training time will set you apart from your peers and help you deliver your own personal brand of excellence.

Intentional Excellence

What we now know from science is that the average footballer can learn to be a lot better than we thought. Research has shown that if we apply ourselves in the right way as we train, we can learn to develop the kind of skill that can improve our game twofold, fivefold, tenfold and maybe more. You can get a lot better than you are now – you can learn to build the game of your dreams.

But the key term here is *'apply yourself in the right way'*. Footballers tend to become fixed and fastened to their current level of play because they don't know how to train effectively. They don't know how to improve. They don't know how to get better.

Developing your game takes willpower and discipline of mind, as much as it does energy and effort. It takes focus and attention to detail. I'm afraid you can't just stride onto the training pitch and run around at warp factor 10. And you can't expect to get better just by turning up.

Now you have a training script, you have to be intentional with it. You have to practice *on purpose*. You have to be deliberate and methodical.

You have to be brave enough to explore movements and body shapes that feel different from your normal game. You have to be bold enough to take risks – to clip a ball over the top when the simple ball would be the safest option, or drill a 40-yard cross-field pass when losing possession will encourage the wrath of your coach.

To improve and improve and improve you have to be brave and bold and courageous and confident. You have to be disciplined and determined. You have to be intense and intentional.

Intentional Practice

Too many footballers train on autopilot. They keep making the same mistakes. They keep the same habits and patterns that hold them back. They remain at the same skill level day after day, month after month, year after year.

You now have a training script – you know exactly what you need to work on. I now want you to flick the autopilot button to off. You're going to train without back-up support and without the aid of brakes. You're going to engage in intentional practice.

Intentional practice is practice on purpose. It's training with improvement in mind. It's not just 'turning up to train and training'. And it's not just training hard! It's training with a series of goals in mind – by having your training script at the forefront of your mind. It's training to improve weaknesses and magnify strengths. It's not necessarily training for perfection, but it *is* training for excellence.

Intentional practice is brain pain. It feels awkward and uncomfortable. It requires stretching away from your comfort zone. What does this *look* like for you? What does this *feel* like? To help you answer this question I'd like to introduce you to my four components of intentional practice. They are:

1. Interesting
2. Intense
3. Internalised
4. Integrated

Let's take you through each one.

Interesting

Intentional practice is interesting. It holds your attention and is absorbing. It sucks you in and keeps you there.

Interest turns up the volume of focus. The brain is constantly scanning the environment for things to lock onto – it will bolt itself tightly to the most important detail at any given time. What you choose to work on must interest you, must be important to you. You must find what you're working on significant to your game in order to focus your full attention on it. This is because attention starts the process of brain change. It starts the process of improvement.

Take a look at your training script before you go out and practice. Sit quietly in the corner of the changing room and stare. Stare at your script and picture its detail.

Stare and picture, stare and picture, stare and picture…

Better still, write your training script on the back of your hand or on your goalkeeper gloves. Inscribe it on your palm or on your wrist so you carry your game improvement programme with you onto the pitch.

At a Premiership club I worked at for several years, I repeatedly had youth team players wrap medical tape around their wrist and asked them to write their script in big, bold letters across the tape. I wanted them to look regularly at what they'd written – between plays, drills and small-sided games. I wanted their memory jolted every few minutes about their purpose out there – to develop, to improve, to learn.

Just by having a training script, you'll increase your level of interest during practice. I think this is vital. I often find that seasoned soccer players, no matter what their level, get bored during training. They switch off and become distracted. They disengage their brain and stop the learning process from taking place. A training script holds your attention and keeps you aware of your game – technically, tactically, mentally and physically – as you practice. There may be nothing more important than this if you want to become a better soccer player.

Intense

Intentional practice is tough to execute. It stretches you and pushes you out of your comfort zone. It demands more from you. It requires an inner voice that energises you and shouts "push".

Intensity isn't just hard work. Intensity is also quality work. Intensity requires a soccer player to keep searching for excellence. If it's your body shape you are working on in your script then you need to maintain the discipline to keep the correct shape throughout training. If you are trying to take more shots in a game then you need to break free from the habit of taking an extra touch or giving in to the temptation of passing the ball, and take more shots – no matter where you are on the park.

When you put brain effort (focused effort) into your training you use up a lot of glucose. Intentional training depletes you of the glucose and sugars that help you concentrate and stay alert. It requires brain power – it can be exhausting. I often say to my players that, after training, physical tiredness should be nothing as compared to the mental fatigue they feel. Brain effort is wearing on both mind and body. Intentional practice should be arduous.

To you, the ambitious soccer player, intensity should mean focus. Get your training script right – get it bang on every second of every minute of every hour. If you're working on your movement to find space then be absorbed by where you are, where the space is, and by anticipating play to drive into that space.

If you're working on catching crosses with greater authority and height then keep your attention on timing your jumps, on getting the biggest lift from the ground that you can, and on taking the ball cleanly and without hesitation.

If you're working on stopping crosses more often, then keep your focus on the process of making it uncomfortable and as difficult as possible for a winger to make the cross.

Focus, attention, concentration, absorption – these are your high priority words and actions when going into a practice session to execute your training script. To improve your soccer you must practice with intensity – your brain must be functioning at a volume that enables you to improve your skills and inch you towards the football of your dreams.

Internalised

You are interested – you have your script to hand at all times. You are intense – your focus of attention is consumed by executing your script. Now become better. How? By *internalising* what you are doing.

Intentional practice requires thought. It's not just action without judgement. That 'just do it' attitude and mindset is more for match day. During training, you should be constantly examining the process of your practice:

- *"Am I keeping my body shape?"*
- *"Did I get into the right position like I wanted to?"*
- *"Have I taken more shots than yesterday?"*
- *"Am I timing my jumps on corners and free kicks better?"*

During intentional practice, you should be evaluating your training script as it unfolds. You should be assessing many of the actions you take and many of the movements you make.

So by 'internalise' I mean – judge what you are doing. I want you to build in small pockets of time during practice to ask yourself how well you are executing your script.

- *"Can I be better?"*
- *"Can I do this with greater intensity?"*
- *"Am I maintaining focus and interest?"*
- *"Am I bang on this at all times?"*
- *"Can I stretch myself more?"*

You *must* be aware of your performance, with relation to what you are trying to accomplish. You must have regular self check-ins that affirm how you are going – you are working hard enough or you are not, you are stretching your comfort zone or you are not, you are sticking to your script or you are not.

Because that is how improvement happens. That is what learning feels like. That is how you are going to develop your skills. You may be at training but are you really present? Are you really engaged? Are you really executing your script? Are you stretching and are you broadening your skill set?

Never ever compromise on these questions. You have to be brutal with yourself. I'd estimate that most footballers never engage in this internalisation process and that is why they fail to keep getting better. You need to be different. You need to keep improving.

Integrated

Are you listening? Are you hearing what your coach has to say? Are you bold and big enough to hear what your teammates have to tell you about your game?

These questions relate to the final 'I' of intentional training – integrated. You must integrate your training with the feedback from others – most importantly, your coaches.

Feedback is a learning fundamental because you can't see yourself train. You need input from others. You need their expertise.

Never, ever see feedback from others, whether it's from the coaching staff or from teammates, as a negative thing. Your attitude towards their voice must be simple and ruthless – "They are trying to help me, they are correcting me, they are supporting my learning as a footballer."

Feedback helps you develop a certainty about your game. It helps you to *know* – "I *know* my body position was wrong there", "I *know* I made the wrong choice of pass", "I *know* I need to get closer to the striker".

It is so important to bring this attitude to the practice pitch. It's so important to *enjoy* criticism and correction. Your trajectory as a soccer player depends on the knowledge and wisdom, the honesty and communication of others.

Choose to enjoy being told that what you did wasn't good enough. You can improve from that honesty. Choose to listen. You can improve when you absorb the words of others who know. Choose to cultivate an attitude of no limits. You can improve when you display that kind of mindset.

Practice with Intention

The quality and efficiency of your training is the biggest determinant of your progress in soccer.

I'm not going to apologise for that belief. Having worked with hundreds of players globally, I know this statement to be true. And it's relevant for every soccer player.

It's true for the Sunday League player who has a nine-to-five job and plays for fun but yearns to emulate his heroes on TV. It's true for the college player who can see the top and just wants to get there. It's true for the lower league footballer whose game touches the greats but who needs to sharpen things to explore just how good he can be. And it's true for the International player who wants to find those small nudges of improvement to win more caps. It's true for everyone.

Technique Number 4

The quality and efficiency of your training is the biggest determinant of your progress in soccer... Engage in intentional training.

5

How Rachel Created
Race Tracks

There was only one thought going through the mind of Rachel Yankey as she lined up in an England shirt for a record 126th time – focus!

26th June 2013, England versus Japan – the Arsenal Ladies striker was about to become the most capped player in English history but her mind was only on the game. It was on her movement and the runs she wanted to make. It was on scoring and assisting. It was on being the best individual and the best team mate she could possibly be.

That mental toughness had started from a young age. Twenty-five years earlier, Rachel Yankey was an eight-year-old girl in love with a game that the boys played. But she hadn't considered it a sport dominated by the opposite sex. There was a ball, a pitch and a couple of goals – what was so difficult about that? She was determined to play and so she did.

When her friends decided to join a local boys' football club she hatched a plan. She shaved her head and called herself Ray (an acronym of her full name – Rachel Aba Yankey). She disguised herself as a boy to get a game of soccer.

And she got away with it for about two years – that's how good she was as a youngster. She didn't look out of place. She wasn't outskilled or outmuscled, she wasn't outpaced or outrun. She experienced dozens of training sessions with boys, many of whom were physically stronger and fleet of foot, and she always kept up with them.

But the fact she wasn't actually a boy was eventually discovered, and with her cover blown she was forced to find a girls' team. She had to move on. But her early experiences playing with her male friends had provided the perfect platform for a future in soccer. It shaped her game, her skills, and her mental toughness.

A Girl Called Ray

Although Rachel Yankey probably wouldn't have been wise to the ways of brain science when she was eight-years-old, the decision she made to play soccer with the boys would have had a profound effect on her life and career.

Imagine it now. Take a peek into the soccer life of an eight-year-old girl striving to keep up with her peers, many of whom were faster and more powerful. She had to learn to be strong in the tackle – shying away would have meant abject failure. She would have been forced to look up more and see more – she needed to be one step ahead to deal with the pace of the game. And she would need to learn the art of body shape to shield the ball, to receive the ball, and to show her presence for the pass. By playing and competing with peers, many of whom were bigger, stronger, and quicker than her – she had shaped a footballing brain to be envious of.

In *Soccer Tough*, I told you the story of former QPR striker Kevin Gallen. I told you how Kevin developed a game worthy of the Premier League by playing countless hours of soccer with his older brothers. Kevin's footballing eyes and feet were enhanced by the constant physical and mental stretching that he endured as he played park football with his siblings.

Just like Kevin, Rachel can point to the hours of park soccer she played with her mates as the starting point for building a soccer game worthy of 126 international caps. The demanding environment she experienced at a young age shaped her inner world and moulded the outer reality of a champion.

Your Inner World: Your Brain

Your inner world is just like a city on earth. It is powered by electricity. It is built for speed. It is designed to constantly communicate no matter what the time – day or night.

Your brain is an incredible piece of machinery. It is more powerful than any computer. It can generate 25 watts of power at any given time – enough to make a lightbulb glow. Over the course of your lifetime, the brain will retain up to one quadrillion bits of information. And it has trillions of tiny connections that inform your behaviour, determine how you think and shape your life. These connections that lie between the billions of cells in your brain, make you the person you are.

You are the footballer you are because of these connections.

Each time you learn something new, you activate different brain cells and create new connections between cells. For example, cells have wired together for the time you have been playing soccer to enable you to kick a ball the way you do and to assess the pitch as quickly as you can. Essentially, the internal structure of your brain is a physical representation of your soccer ability. Your soccer brain is your soccer game! When you learn a new skill you create new connections – your brain literally changes its structure.

This process gets to the heart of growth in football. Your brain wiring is powerful. There are more connections in your brain than there are stars in the universe. Information crosses these connections at approximately 268 miles per hour allowing us to think and act effectively, and move and behave appropriately. Improving and developing your football is a simple process of creating new connections between cells in your brain. And what we now know in brain science is that the brain can continue to establish new connections (and learn) for the whole of your life. It may be easier to learn when you're younger but it's still very possible to keep learning throughout the whole of adulthood. Thus no matter what your age, you *can* improve your football. You *can* ingrain new skills and new tactical plays.

When Rachel Yankey used to play soccer with the boys, she was furiously connecting the billions of tiny connections in her brain. And because this footballing landscape was so challenging, the connections she was making were becoming super thick and super fast. She got better quicker! Just by striving to keep up with her peers, she was upgrading her inner computer every single day. And by being forced to find the kind of techniques and the standard of skills that would help her match or beat her young rivals she was pushed to try new things.

She was forced to experiment. She was forced to practice and train as effectively as she could. She was on a road to excellence.

The Road to Excellence

There is a useful 'road' analogy I use with soccer players to explain this brain wiring process.

When you start learning a new skill, the connections between cells are small and weak. At this stage, you are building pathways (think of a narrow, weed-strewn country pathway). Signals between cells at this stage are slow (after all, you can't race a car down a narrow pathway, you can only stroll down one). Executing the new skill is challenging – you have to really think about what you're doing as you're doing it.

When Rachel started playing with her male friends, her footballing brain consisted of pathways. A path for passing. A path for shooting. A path for controlling the ball.

After a little bit of practice your pathways start to become stronger and roads start to form. Signals become more powerful and speed up. The skill starts to evolve – it feels more natural and more comfortable. You no longer feel like you've been asked to write with your weaker hand.

As Rachel played more and more with her peers, the roads in her brain would have started to form. As she practiced for hours on end, she would have seen a noticeable improvement in her game. Her soccer brain was growing and with it, her skills would have been developing – seeing more, doing more, quicker to the ball, anticipating things more accurately.

As you continue to practice, your new technique becomes commonplace in your game. It can be executed smoothly, efficiently and effectively. At this stage, you've turned the roads into motorways. Connections are stronger (think of the reinforcement of a motorway) and quicker (think of the higher speed limit on a highway).

By playing with mostly bigger and stronger players Rachel's hand would have been forced. Play with intelligence or lose the ball. Compete with positioning and movement in mind or never get the ball.

By playing soccer with the boys' team, she would have learnt to find solutions to difficult situations. She would have developed her vision and awareness for space, for movement and for anticipation. Park football would have established a set of brain connections that were ready to develop into motorways.

The world's best players are the ones who have race tracks in their brain. Their levels of practice and training have developed connections that are thick and insulated and the speed with which messages travel across brain cells is rapid. They have these speedy connections for every part of their game – tackling, passing, shooting, positional awareness, catching (for a goalkeeper), trapping and controlling the ball. This is how they make the complex look simple.

As Rachel moved on to her teenage years and into her twenties, she started to play with Arsenal Women's team and with the England International team. Her brain connections would have thickened and super fast messages would have started to shoot through like lightning bolts. It would have taken some time but she would have developed race tracks in her brain.

Pathways to roads to motorway to race tracks. Where are the skills in your game right now?

I love this analogy because, to my mind, not only does it de-mystify the art of learning, it also presents the possibility of improvement. I abhor the notion that my skill set will stay static forever. I want to go on learning, developing and improving. And the neurological evidence I have presented to you, above, albeit simplistic, helps me to believe that you can turn that ambition into reality. You *can* become a better, more skilful footballer. You *can* become more knowledgeable about tactics. You *can* improve your tactical play. An old dog can *always* learn new tricks!

But just because you 'can' doesn't mean that it's easy. It wasn't easy for Rachel. It wasn't easy for Xavi or Gareth Bale or Ibrahimovic.

Don't let my simple driving analogy fool you into thinking it will be easy. Turning paths into race tracks requires more than just hard work. Some say repetition is the mother of skill. I say repetition is only its potential parent. It is the *quality* of your practice more than the quantity that establishes keen connections between cells. It is vital to read and re-read the last few chapters so you know what your training script is and you are ready to practice with intention. You are must be ready to train deliberately. Quality, focused practice makes brain cells hungry to connect.

Hungry Connections

It is your training script, combined with intentional training that helps you connect your brain cells, build skill and improve your tactical execution. Fixing your script firmly in your mind, as you go out to train, and then adhering to the 4 I's of intentional training will change your brain and ultimately change your game – for the better. Recall the 4 I's…

1. Interesting
2. Intense
3. Internalised
4. Integrated

To feed your hungry connections, I'd like you to try this visualisation exercise as you work on your script during training. Picture an inner movie of your brain cells connecting up. As you practice more and more, imagine your pathways turning into roads and then motorways. Conjure up an image of your brain cells firing at lightning speed so the connections thicken and become stronger until you have race tracks growing throughout your brain.

- With every touch of the ball you are creating race tracks
- Every run you make creates race tracks
- Every time you look up and around, you are creating race tracks
- Every time you act with speed on what you've just seen, you are creating race tracks
- Every pass you make creates race tracks
- Every catch you hold creates race tracks
- Every first touch out of your feet creates race tracks
- Every time you jump with strength, you are creating race tracks

You have a bottomless pit of potential. You have a training script. You know how to practice with intention. Now go create race tracks for every part of your game!

Technique Number 5

Create Race Tracks for Every Part of Your Game.

6

Reach for Ronaldo, Stretch for Smith

Let me be very clear.

I'm not saying that everyone who reads this book will lift the World Cup, play Champions League, compete as a professional, get a college scholarship, or represent their County or State team. That's not what I'm saying. How far someone goes in the beautiful game is determined by many factors, some of which are out of your control.

Incredible ability has fallen by the wayside for many reasons – injury, life distractions, a lack of opportunity, bad performances at the wrong time, and sometimes because of plain old bad luck.

I have worked with some players over the years who have shown incredible physical ability, who have enormous dedication, and who have worked diligently on their mindset – but sustained an injury at the wrong time or who have simply lost a little form when their chance to impress was at its highest.

Success in soccer, as it is in life, is complicated! It's not straightforward.

But let me tell you something that I believe *is* straightforward. Something that is, to me, a non-negotiable and a critical essential. Soccer players must reach for their playing dreams and stretch their comfort zone. Soccer players must reach and stretch relentlessly. Soccer players must reach for the best in the world and stretch for their optimal ability no matter who they are and no matter what level they compete at. By doing so, they give themselves the very best opportunity to discover just how good they can be.

They must reach for Ronaldo. That awareness, that first touch, that intelligence, that work ethic, that heading, that movement off the ball and that delivery. They must reach for the World Player of the Year – what does that look like? What does that feel like? What is he thinking on the pitch? What is he seeing? How is he formulating his next move?

They must stretch for Smith – Kelly Smith, one of the greatest players ever to put on soccer boots. That power, that control, that anticipation, that hunger, that shooting. Over 100 caps for the English National team – what does that look like? What does that feel like? What is she thinking on the pitch? What is she seeing? How is she formulating her next move?

They must reach for Ronaldo and they must stretch for Smith. Every soccer player must reach and stretch for the elite – for the best in the world in their position.

Reach and stretch, reach and stretch. Abby Wambach, Yaya Toure, Christine Sinclair, Gareth Bale, Louisa Necib,

Reach and stretch, reach and stretch. Manuel Neuer, Nadine Angerer, Vincent Kompany, Marta, Philipp Lahm...

What do they see? How have they improved themselves as players? What does space mean to them? How much effort do they exert? How do they talk to themselves as they compete? What are they thinking as they warm up? What level of intensity produces their best? How do they relax before a game?

The trajectory of your soccer may well be determined by the quality of the questions you ask yourself about the games of your models. It may well be determined by the answers you furnish your own game with.

Reach and stretch, reach and stretch, reach and stretch.

Seeing Possibility

Can everyone become Ronaldo or Kelly Smith or another world-class player? Probably not. But that doesn't mean you don't strive to become the best. That doesn't mean you don't try. A footballer will surprise herself daily with the progress she is making when she puts her dreams and ambitions at the forefront of her mind.

Every great soccer player sees possibility in his game and possibility in his hero's game. He *stares* and *steals* and *stretches*.

He *stares* at his role model – someone who plays a few levels or many levels above him – and he marches a relentless beat towards the game of his idol.

He looks at the German goalkeeper Manuel Neuer and sees the strong leap off the ground, the pinpoint perfect timing of a jump that has him soar above the opposition strikers. And he sees Neuer catch and hold the ball like it's a new born baby – like it's his baby – like he *owns* the ball, and it is no-one else's.

He makes a decision about the skills in Neuer's play that he wants to *steal* from the great goalkeeper. Then this soccer player stretches. He fixes his focus firmly on developing the actions and movements that help Neuer catch a crossing ball.

You have to reach and stretch, reach and stretch

If you are a defender, you may choose to look at Ali Krieger, the American World Cup winner.

Look and stare, look and stare. Look at her positioning, stare at her movement, look at how she checks opposition and ball. Stare at how she times her tackles to perfection. Look and stare, look and stare.

A midfielder could look at Toni Kroos, the German and Real Madrid footballer. He could look and stare, look and stare. Kroos shows strength, movement, awareness, positioning. He shows will and want. He portrays confidence and assuredness. Look and stare, look and stare.

What you see and reflect on in your brain plays an important role in your progress as a soccer player. This is because your brain has mirrors. When you watch you shape your brain. By projecting a strong, vivid image of excellence through your eyes you start to sculpt the games of model players into your mind.

Look and stare, look and stare then reach and stretch, reach and stretch

The Imagination of a Champion

The soccer players who reach and stretch on a daily basis not only carve out the kind of skills that separate the best from the rest, they also create a mental blueprint that helps them manage the emotional ups and downs that soccer delivers.

I've worked with young players who have been dropped from their Under 12 team because they were deemed not big or strong enough. I've worked with Premier League Academy scholars who have been released because the coaching staff didn't see a future for them at the very top level of the game. And I've worked with amateur footballers (players who compete for fun but who take the game seriously) who have made terrible mistakes leading to goals that have relegated their team or have lost cup matches.

My message to them is reach and stretch. You keep reaching and stretching. Nothing and no-one stops you from improving. Nothing and no-one diverts your focus away from your bottomless pit of potential.

Stuff happens in football. Mistakes are made. Own goals are conceded. Easy opportunities are missed. No matter, just keep reaching and stretching.

This is what the English striker Carlton Cole did when his career was taking a downward turn (there is more about my work with Carlton Cole in *Soccer Tough*). When he found himself in the reserve team for West Ham he decided enough was enough. He had seen his career go from a very promising youngster in the Chelsea first team to a striker who was struggling for any game time at all.

Carlton decided to reach and stretch. He worked every day in the gym and he analysed his game with then West Ham manager Gianfranco Zola. He spoke with me on a weekly basis to improve his mindset and he took time after every training session to practice his skills.

After just a few months, his reaching and stretching started to pay off. He won a place in the first team and he started to score goals. And just shy of 18 months into his newfound commitment, he won a place in the England international team. He made his debut against Spain, the World Champions at the time.

Carlton could have chosen to give up. He could have chosen to play in the West Ham reserves and spend his career wondering what could have been. He didn't. He decided to reach and stretch to see just how good he could be. In my eyes he found his personal brand of excellence – he became a champion.

Champion sports competitors balance the vision they have for their game in the now and the future. They place one eye on the present striving to compete as best they can every day in training and every week on match day. But they have the other eye directed towards the future – reaching and stretching towards their hero, their idol, their model, their future perfect.

No matter what happens on the pitch, you carry on. Win or lose you carry on. You carry on reaching. You carry on stretching. That is what champions do. That is what Gold Medal performances are made of. That is the only way you can truly discover how much ability you really have, and how good you can really become!

Technique Number 6

Reach and Stretch Relentlessly!

Practice Pep Talk

You have to train, you have to play and you have to think like there are no limits to your ability.

Do you think – when you start to do this – that you'll hold yourself the same as before? Do you think you'll act the same? When you ingrain the belief that you have a bottomless pit of potential, do you think you'll talk to yourself in the same way?

When you start to train, to play and to think like there are no limits to your ability then you'll conduct yourself differently on and off the pitch. Your self-belief will rise higher and fall slower. Your focus will stabilise and distractions will shift quicker. Destructive emotions will flat-line and your perseverance will strengthen.

You have to train, you have to play and you have to think like there are no limits to your ability.

*

To be the best you can be you have to profile the next level.

It's not enough to immerse yourself in a no-limits mentality. You have to live it and breathe it and sleep it. This means taking a long, hard and honest look at your current game. Ask yourself the tough question: "What does better look like?" Examine your strengths and borrow from the best – champions of tomorrow learn from the champions of today.

Write down a template for your future game – set your course for success. It's one thing to want it, it's another thing to put into practice *exactly* what you have to do to get to your destination. Being a student of *the* game and a student of *your* game is motivation wrapped in a layer of intelligence – you need to know what you need to magnify and what you need to improve.

To be the best you can be, you have to profile the next level.

*

To reach your own version of personal excellence, you have to design your training script and take small steps every month to build the game of your dreams.

Once you've profiled the next level, and compiled the evidence, you can build your training script. A script is a narrowed focus – it's a smaller version of your profile and it encompasses the specific areas you're going to work on for the coming month.

The champions in sport do this. They breakdown their game to the exact components they need to improve then they take to the training pitch or court or course and take action.

I want this for your game. I want you to go and execute. I want you to go and get better. Go and train and go and practice with passion, with precision, and with a vision directed towards perfection.

To be the best you can be, you have to design your training script and take small steps every month to build the game of your dreams.

*

The quality and efficiency of your training is the biggest determinant of your progress in soccer.

Train deliberately. Train on purpose. Train with intention.

Practicing with intensity is not enough. You have to take ownership of your training script by focusing your mind tightly on improving the skills you want to improve. This will be uncomfortable at first, but that's okay. The art of becoming better is to shift the uncomfortable into the zone of comfortable. The art of improving is to over-think a skill until you do it automatically and naturally.

Getting better at your soccer is as a result of combining focus, commitment, drive and comfort-busting action.

The quality and efficiency of your training is the biggest determinant of your progress in soccer.

*

Create race tracks for *every* part of your game.

Your brain is the electricity charging your improvement programme, and your inner world is a representation of your outer reality. Whenever you take to the practice pitch – to train with intention – you are wiring your brain for excellence. You are turning pathways into roadways into motorways and finally into race tracks.

Your goal should be simple – create race tracks for *every* part of your game. Train your script with the intention to build race tracks for your ball control. Build race tracks for your positional awareness. Build race tracks for your movement. Build for your first touch, for your tackling, for your passing. Build and build and build those race tracks.

Create race tracks for every part of your game.

*

Reach and stretch relentlessly.

A champion craves to become the best she can possibly be. She is hungry for better.

If you win – get better. If you lose – get better. If you're subbed – get better. If you are coming back from injury – get better. If you're towards the end of your footballing career – get better. If you've been released from a club – get better. If you've had a terrible training session – get better.

A champion aches for better. She has a vision of improvement that pierces her mind and fires her belly.

If you've lost the final – get better. If you've had a shocking performance – get better. If the coach says "Not good enough" – get better. If a team mate digs you out – get better. If you have no winners' medals – get better.

Reach and stretch, reach and stretch, reach and stretch for your dream game.

Reach and stretch relentlessly.

Prepare – Introduction

You cannot force a great game. You cannot force a win. Performances are often made or broken in the lead up to a match, and your mindset during those days, hours and minutes before you grace the pitch is as important as it is during the competition itself.

World-class preparation begins with knowledge. It starts by knowing exactly what you have to do to give yourself the very best chance to compete at your peak. In football, you win in your mind first, then you go play. There can be no shortcuts. You must demand detail and you must stress the small things. They matter.

Soccer players are accustomed to warming up their bodies for play but I want more for you and your football. I want you to become the very best in the world at warming up your mindset. I want you to fine-tune your mental game in the lead up to a match. I want you to turn up the volume of focus and confidence whilst maintaining the appropriate balance between intensity and relaxation.

In this section, you'll learn how to:

- Prime your confidence and stock up on energy
- Have a specific individual plan for the match ahead
- Get ready to manage yourself on the pitch
- Create pictures in your mind without fuss and without deliberation
- Have a routine for matchday – one that builds and stores excellence

In this section, I'm going to introduce you to a different language. Too many soccer players obsess over shooting, ball control and tackling without a passion for the thoughts and attitudes that underpin consistent high performance. I want my language to become your passion. I want you to embrace the concept of energy and confidence bars. I want you to be lightning quick on your self-talk and body controllers. I want you charging your inner batteries on a weekly basis.

I hope these new ideas excite and inspire you. I hope they lead to the sensational soccer you dream of. So let's prepare to play!

7

Raising the Bars

Football is a feeling. It's an emotion, a mood, a sensation that rips through your body. It's a vibe, an air, an aura, a bodily instinct.

Sometimes you take to the pitch and all of those inner qualities are positive and helpful and constructive. Sometimes you feel unbeatable and indestructible. Other times you cross the white line and you feel negative – your spirit is low, your internal experience destructive.

Football is a feeling and I'd like you to feel it now. Put yourself on the pitch into the position you favour; add a ball, your team mates and an opposition into the mix. And play…

Play with the feelings you want to experience. Play with a feeling of focus, and with a feeling of freedom. Play with a feeling of commitment and decisiveness. Play feeling sharp and lively and upbeat and alert and alive and ready.

Make this private screening as realistic as you can – allow those feelings to swirl through your body as your brain projects pictures of your fantasy game.

See it and feel it. Make it big and bold and bright. Add a soundtrack if you like.

Now I want you to stop. Stop your personal movie and let the screen go black. Let your mind settle for 30 seconds then start another game of fantasy football. This time I want you to reverse the feelings you experienced in your last blockbuster. This time I want you to inject the kind of unhelpful and destructive feelings you might experience during a poor performance.

This time I want you to play with lethargy. Play flatfooted, in a bad mood, slow, uncommitted and flustered. Play with feelings of worry, doubt and anxiety. Play feeling as if your feet are sticky, your voice mute and your vision narrowed. Play with feelings of panic and fear and distraction.

Just because this time I have asked you to imagine a negative scene doesn't mean I don't want you to get a rich, vivid experience. I still want you to shoot the appropriate feelings through your body, legs and feet. I still want this imprinted on your brain and nervous system.

Make all your images – even these negative ones – big and bold and bright. Your education as a soccer player must include a microscopic look at what lays you low as a player, just as much as what helps you fly.

The Fragility of Feeling

Your external sensations – the speed of your boots, the sharpness in your movement, the penetration of the runs you make, your ability to find space and use that space – are all heavily influenced by how you feel going into a game.

Having worked with hundreds of soccer players, I believe there are two primary feelings that impact and influence a player's performance – your feelings of confidence and your feelings of energy.

To my mind, confidence is a feeling. Take a little time to reflect back on a game when you played at your best (or close to your best). No doubt you were confident, but where did that confidence come from? Where did you experience that sensation of confidence?

When you open up that inner picture book of you, at your best, I think you'll find that the confidence is spread throughout your body. From head to toe, it flows and surges through your muscles and your joints.

- The feeling of confidence through your feet – lightness – like you're treading on hot coals and you don't want to burn yourself

- The feeling of confidence through your legs – decisive – every pass reaching its target and every shot struck cleanly and with power
- The feeling of confidence though your hips – mobility – swerving, shifting and twisting into the right body shape to shield, protect and open up
- The feeling of confidence through your stomach – certainty – every action, every motion executed with assuredness and security
- The feeling of confidence through your chest – strength – desire, determination, discipline
- The feeling of confidence through your head – focus – eyes quickly shifting between the ball, your team mates, the opposition, and the space

Just like confidence, energy is also a feeling. Being relentless is a feeling. Urging yourself on is a feeling. Driving yourself forward in that last lung-busting ten minutes is a feeling. A footballer *feels* dynamic. A footballer *feels* strong. A footballer *feels* vigorous.

In contrast, a soccer player may *feel* lethargic. She may *feel* slow or sluggish or tired or lazy. "I just wasn't feeling it today" is something I hate to hear, but a statement that is said to me all too often. It is one of the most destructive sentences that soccer players let loose from their lips. It is a problem every footballer must find a solution for.

Answers need to be acquired to combat a lacklustre feeling because every performance requires energy. It is a non-negotiable in any sport, let alone the demanding non-stop environment of a game of football. Every move, every motion you take must be performed with high energy.

This energy is built from fitness but is reinforced by the thoughts you have and the actions you take on a moment-by-moment and hour-to-hour basis. Get little sleep and you find yourself de-energised. Eat the wrong food and you'll feel like you're lacking in energy. Over-train and your feelings of energy will reduce.

Confidence and energy are feelings that are collected from many sources. They are fashioned by how you direct your attention within you, and the behaviours you display to the world outside of you. And I have a powerful technique that can help you prepare your confidence and energy stores for your upcoming game.

Your Personal Playstation Bars

Let's make this nice and simple to visualise.

Most of you (if not all of you) who are reading this book will have played Playstation or Xbox games. Many of these games incorporate something like an energy bar or a life bar to monitor your ability to sustain actions (and to stay alive!). Most classic action or sports based games (for example, Street Fighter) have something like this as a gauge to know just how well you are doing.

I'd like you to introduce something similar into your soccer. I'd like you to imagine you have two bars going into your next match – a confidence bar and an energy bar.

As part of your match preparation, you need to know what you need to do to raise your confidence and energy bars to their highest possible point. You need to know the habits and actions that are going to help you feel as confident as possible and as energised as possible.

Throughout this section of the book, I will be returning to this idea of confidence and energy bars, and in the next section, we will explore techniques to help you sustain the bars as you compete. For now, I want you to start to think about what you have to do to build up your bars so you can feel great going into a match and give yourself a chance to play to the very best of your ability.

Finding Your Bar Markers

By the end of this book, I'd like you to become fluent in your personal bar markers.

By markers, I am talking about the thoughts you need to familiarise yourself with and the actions you have to experience in order to raise your confidence and energy bars to the highest of heights.

Let me take you through a few now. Remember, some of these will be familiar to you. Others will be introduced to you later in the book – so don't panic!

Confidence Markers Examples

- Picturing my best games every day for five minutes
- Taking 25 dead ball free kicks at the end of every training session
- Going to the gym twice a week to work on strength
- Work one-to-one with a skills trainer once a week
- Always reflect on my strengths after every training session
- Keep great body language at the training ground at all times
- Watch YouTube clips of my role model twice a week
- Picture my match script everyday
- Know exactly what I'm going to do if I make a few mistakes in the match
- Be intentional with my training

Energy Markers Examples

- Going to the gym three times a week – running 5k as quickly as possible
- Protein shakes daily
- 8 hours sleep a night minimum
- Keep my self-talk positive on a daily basis (spot the ANTs and squash them quickly)
- Set monthly outcome goals to keep me motivated
- Get away from soccer as often as possible (stay mentally fresh)
- Appropriate carb load two hours before playing
- Strive to knock any arguments with team mates on the head as quickly as possible – no negatives between myself and team mates
- Relaxation exercise for ten minutes a day – experience clear-mindedness regularly

- Mentally and physically relax the morning of a game – take my mind away from play until 2 hours before kick off

Making Your Choices

Above, I have written 10 example markers for both confidence and energy bars. I'd like you to try to come up with five confidence markers and five energy markers. If you're struggling for five then get at least three for each – you can always build on them later.

Make them as meaningful to yourself, and your game, as possible. For example, an adult amateur footballer who plays county or district soccer may have a maximum alcohol intake per week marker to increase energy levels. Players at this level, and this age group, may also have a marker restricting the amount of other sport he or she plays to maintain daily energy. However, young players competing at an age when sport specialisation is unhelpful will probably bolster their confidence and energy by playing more sport and by competing in a variety of activities.

Many of my players have their confidence bars filled with markers connected to training. Their feelings of confidence skyrockets on matchday when they know they've trained intentionally and when they know they are on course with their training script. When they've stretched themselves on the training ground, they know they can trust their game going into a competitive situation.

Similarly, the soccer players I work with, tend to bolster their energy bar through healthy lifestyles and positive relationships. They strive to be fitter than their team mates, better nourished, and in better physical shape than anyone else going into every match. But they also know the importance and value of rest and recuperation. They know that energy levels on match day require plenty of time away from soccer, physically and mentally.

Raising Your Bars

What are the five markers that will help you cross the white line feeling full of confidence? What five markers will help you to conserve enough energy to fuel your presence on the pitch?

Of course, there may be many markers on your notepad, but I think it's useful to write down your top five and make sure they become part of a checklist you keep to with unbending regularity.

It is so often the unseen things that champions do that make them champions – the actions, no matter how small, that they commit to on a daily basis that separates them from those who finish a few milliseconds, or a single point, or a solitary goal behind them. Promising yourself that you'll complete your markers every week isn't enough – you have to do them. You have to carry them out. You have to live them.

This kind of commitment gives your body permission to run onto the pitch with confidence and energy, and carrying a brain that's clear minded and well fuelled.

This is how you start to prepare for a match – the kind of preparation that will have you feeling electric with energy and crackling with confidence.

Technique Number 7

Raise your confidence and energy bars daily.

8

Getting into Process

What is your goal going into a game?

What desired outcome do you burn into your temples before you stride onto the pitch? What objective fires the rockets in your boots?

I ask these questions because what you try to achieve in a match massively influences the thoughts you have on the pitch. In other words, the feelings that you experience and the performances you deliver. The targets you set yourself matter.

In fact, one of the first questions I ask new clients relates to the aims they set themselves for each and every game. *"What is your objective? What targets do you have?"*

The answers I receive are inconsistent. They range from players having no goals at all through to targets that damage confidence, motivation and focus. Both can be as bad as each other – an absence of goals *and* the wrong goals can kill your game before you set foot on the pitch.

And this is the extraordinary thing about the mental side of soccer. Set the wrong objectives on a Wednesday for a Saturday game and you diminish your chances of being at your best at the weekend. Ignore the process of match day goal setting altogether and your once a week match is in danger of being a flop.

You've got to set goals for your upcoming game. And they've got to be the right goals.

Your Relationship with Football

Have a think about the kind of goals and objectives you can set yourself. Let me tell you about some of the ones I hear regularly.

- "I want to win"
- "I want to score"
- "I want to keep a clean sheet"
- "I want to play my best"
- "I want to complete all my passes"

These are the kind of targets that the players I work with tell me when I first meet them. I admire them. They are a sign of competitiveness. They demonstrate want and will. They are the type of objectives that TV commentators would have us believe bear the hallmark of champions. Winners want to win right? They want to be at their best, yes? They ache for maximum points, lots of goals scored, and few conceded.

But despite my respect for these goals I don't believe they are the best objectives to set. In fact, they can be destructive to the ambitious footballer. I understand that statement might sound a little strange. You may think the best goal a striker can have is to score. You may believe that a goalkeeper should have a goal of keeping a clean sheet.

Why do you think I might disagree with these objectives? Before you read on have a think. Why do you think I might insist on my clients setting different targets? Now let me explain…

In simple terms, the goals I've written above are outcome and performance objectives. Outcome and performance targets are poor ones to have come matchday. And I'll give you several reasons why:

1. They are obvious – I know as a striker that my job is to score and I know as a goalkeeper my job is to keep a clean sheet. There isn't an individual on a team who doesn't want to win. Outcome and performance targets are there no matter what, so

there is no need to set these types of goals. They are achieved as a consequence of other factors.

2. They can lead to doubt. If, at the forefront of my mind, rests the objective of scoring, and I haven't scored by the 80th minute of play, the volume of worry can increase in my mind and rip uncertainty through my body. "I'm not going to score today" can become your inner voice.

3. They can lead to despondency. If a goalkeeper has the goal of keeping a clean sheet yet concedes a goal early on, it will become difficult for him to deal with this emotionally. He has already failed in his objective. He has already lost!

4. They can negatively affect your game. If a midfielder has a goal of completing all of her passes then she will likely avoid risk. She will pass backwards. She won't pass with progression. She won't send dangerous balls in behind the defence. Playing timidly, she'll reduce the freedom in her actions and motions.

5. Above all, you can't completely control outcome and performance. You can influence both but you can't control them. As a striker you can play a great game (and grab some crucial assists) but still not score. A defender may defend for her life, put in some outstanding tackles and show accomplished positional awareness, but still be on the losing side. A goalkeeper may pull off a couple of world class saves but still concede two.

I want you to re-read the five reasons I've given. Then read them again. Drill them into your mind so they stick to your footballing brain. I don't want you setting these goals – they are the silent assassins of great football. They kill excellence.

Allow me to furnish you with a very important fact about soccer and mindset:

Winning, scoring goals, playing at your best and keeping clean sheets – these will take care of themselves. You can't control them and you don't need to worry about them. You can't force them and they don't need to play on your mind. They can cause you to play tight, tense and timidly. They can create anxiety – specifically doubt and worry. They can trigger the first drips of despondency. You don't need to focus on them.

I'm going to force your arm here a little. I want you to have a different match day focus to the ordinary soccer player. I want you to have a different inner story entering the stadium. You need a better, more effective relationship with soccer provided by a different set of goals, targets and objectives.

The Process

If you want to be the very best soccer player you can be, you need a sophisticated way of thinking about soccer. You need a sophisticated *relationship* with football.

- Taking your mind away from winning doesn't mean you shrink away from glory
- Taking your mind away from scoring doesn't mean you'll leave the pitch empty handed
- Taking your mind away from performing at your best for your team mates doesn't mean you will let them down

In fact, it is quite the opposite.

A footballer who immerses herself in the *process* of scoring gives herself a better chance to score more. A soccer player who is engrossed in the *process* of defending gives his team a greater chance of keeping the opposition goalless. A player who throws herself at the *process* will likely be a great individual and a great team mate. She will give herself and her team mates the very best chance of winning.

So what is this thing called process?

Scripting Your Process

The process is the *how* of performance. It refers to the characteristics, attitudes, behaviours, actions and ways of thinking that drive performance.

What drives your performance? What are the responsibilities within your role on the pitch?

The process can be as simple or as complex as you like. It can be one word or it can be a series of short sentences. It must be specific to you – your strengths, the areas you want to improve, and the responsibilities within your role. It can vary from match to match and, although stability with your process is useful, I imagine you will change it depending on the opposition in front of you, the time of the season and what you're working on in your training script. If you're very young, you may choose to condense your process down to just one thought or idea. As you advance your football, you can make the process longer and more complex (although most of the clients I work with, at the very top level of the game, keep the process short and concise).

To make things as simple as possible for clients I stopped using the term 'process' many years ago. I think it sounds too much like science – only sport psychologists use that term. So, instead of talking to players about their process I talk to them about their 'match script'.

I use the term 'script' for three reasons:

1. It's easy to remember and catchy
2. Script is a shortened term for prescription – I like that idea – "What is your prescription for the game?"
3. A script relates to acting, and as we will go on to discuss, in this section of the book, a competitive performance in soccer is just like an act. For every game you play, you need a script and you have to act out that script (but more on that later).

So, let's make this simple and clear – your goal for a game of soccer is to go and execute your script; the performance and outcome will take care of themselves. Let me repeat that – your goal for a game of soccer is to go and execute your script; performance and outcome will take care of themselves. Here are some examples of match scripts:

Goalkeeper Script

1. Vocal at all times

2. Get into set position quickly
3. Aggressive in the air

Defender Script

1. Stand winger up
2. Always show the outside
3. Body shape on corners

Midfielder Script

1. Quick to close down (cut off space)
2. Strong in every challenge
3. Play head up (spot the gaps)

Winger Script

1. Brave with runs – take players on
2. Send balls into the danger area
3. Find the far post as often as possible

Striker Script

1. Relentless runs
2. Bring defenders in deep
3. Focus on a great strike

What do the plays in these scripts have in common? They are all related to the characteristics, behaviours and ways of thinking that help players execute the responsibilities within their role. But most crucially they are controllable. There are no plays that rely on external factors that are outside a footballer's control.

- *I can't guarantee scoring but I can choose to make runs that give me the best chance of scoring*
- *I can't guarantee keeping a clean sheet but I can choose to be aggressive in the air*
- *I can't guarantee completing all my passes but I can choose to play head up and pass with confidence*

So what are the contents of *your* match script? What two or three plays underpin an outstanding performance? Take some time to think about what your coach wants from you. What does your role demand? What have you done in the past that's been successful?

In my experience, a match script often includes plays related to:

- Movement
- Runs
- Awareness
- Positional discipline
- Tackling, passing, shooting and heading
- Ball control
- Shape
- Working forward and back
- Body language
- Self-talk
- Vocals
- Decision making

These are just a few categories that could form the basis of plays for a match script. But there is another way to form a very simple match script – a simple script, but a powerful script.

Simplifying Your Script

I want you to take your mind elsewhere for a couple of minutes. We're going to exercise your memory and your imagination.

Firstly, I'd like you to think about you at your very best. What did that look like? What did that feel like? What did others see when you were outstanding?

Play out that match again – this time in your mind. Make your inner images big and bold and bright. Crank up the volume of the emotion you felt at the time. Play in full colour. Play from your own eyes and from the side of the pitch.

What words would you use to sum up how you played? Determined? Committed? Athletic? Focused? I want you to swirl the words you think of around in your mind – let's give you some more:

Confident, sharp, dominant, alert, alive, lively, strong, belief, toes, upbeat, positive, ready, relaxed, tall, decisive.

What did your best game look like? Feel like? Picture you at your very best.

Now I want you to change the scene. I'd like you to do a similar exercise only this time I want you to picture your perfect performance. I want you to envision your dream game. Not just a 10/10 performance, but a 12/10 match. Be as unrealistic as you like. Play around with your inner pictures and direct them at super speed, with super strength and with super intensity. Feel wave after wave of positive emotion flood through your body from head to foot.

What does your dream game look like? What does it feel like?

What words relate to your fantasy game? Brave? Bold? Cool? Free? Allow those words to whirl and swish and swoop around your mind – let's give you some more:

Relentless, loud, impactful, big, energy, powerful, dynamic, active, disciplined, non-stop, ruthless, controlled.

I want you to pick three words that represent a combination of your best game and your dream game. Make sure they are words that are action-based and preferably emotive words – words that inspire you, that drive you and that are related to your role on the pitch.

Here are some examples:

- Energetic, strong, focused
- Belief, committed, brave
- Relentless, toes, relaxed
- Calm, bold, big

Don't pick key words that you think will suit others or which are related to the style and play of another soccer player – your key words must be personal to you.

When you say them to yourself, they must open up a catalogue of inner pictures that relate to the plays, the behaviours, the attitudes and the responsibilities you want to execute within your role. They must excite you. They must energise you. When you reflect on them, you should feel a tingle of excellence run through your body. When you say them out loud, you must be able to feel the thump of your heart pound against your chest.

These key words are you at your best. These key words are a supercharged you. These key words are a superior you – a superior you that will make the opposition inferior.

Throw in an Animal

Now I'm going to ask you a bit of a strange question, but I want you to go with it.

When you think of your best game and your dream game, and when you think about performing in the style of your three words, is there an animal that comes to mind?

It might be a lion, king of the jungle, loud and proud; or a cheetah, lightning fast and super agile; or your animal could be an ape or a gorilla. It might be a snake or panther, a monkey or a greyhound. I want you to choose an animal that relates to your words, to your best game and your dream game.

Those of you who got stuck into the first *Soccer Tough* book will recognise this question. This is the animal technique I used to help Anthony Stokes get his dream move to Celtic. Stokesy became a greyhound as he competed. He envisioned and then executed the kind of intensity, energy and never say die attitude that a greyhound displays on a daily basis. He made himself a nightmare for defenders, constantly moving, constantly striving to find space, constantly working to fill the gaps between defenders.

Although it sounds very strange, relating your soccer to an animal is really useful and is connected to how we learn and function as human beings. In psychology, we call it a 'visual metaphor'. The brain loves to convert verbal information into visual images to make learning and understanding easy.

'Being' an animal on the pitch can echo in our mind. It's meaningful – we know that a lion is big and strong and powerful and we know that we know that we want to be big and strong and powerful on the pitch. We know that a cheetah is fast, a predator and athletic – we know that we want to be fast, a predator and athletic on the pitch.

Animals are super human. When you picture a greyhound you think relentless and no stopping. When you think of a snake, you picture quick and invisible and cunning. When you think of a panther, you think of sly and brutal and speedy. Animals can equate to you at your best or you fitting into your dream game. They can amplify your key words.

I'd like you to affix one or two key words to your animal. Here's some examples:

- Dominant greyhound
- Confident lion
- Quick, lively snake
- Focused, relentless monkey
- Energetic, confident panther

These are great additions to your script. They create powerful pictures that spike your nervous system into action. Allowing those pictures to revolve in your mind daily is an outstanding way to prepare to perform. And then leaving the changing room to these inner sketches will boost your confidence and power up your focus.

When you add them to the script they must be a part of you. You must *become* a confident lion – what does that look like, what does that feel like? You must *become* a dominant greyhound – what does that look like, what does that feel like? You must *become* an energetic, confident panther – what does that look like, what does that feel like?

And as we shall go on to discuss in the next section of this book –
nothing and no-one takes you away from confident lion. Nothing and
no-one takes you away from dominant greyhound. Nothing and no-one
takes you away from energetic, confident panther. Nothing and no-one
takes you away from your script.

If the animal technique really doesn't work for you that's fine. There is
something else you can attach your key words to.

And Your Role Model

If the animal technique just doesn't quite create the right pictures in
your mind, and isn't quite meaningful enough, then we can work on
something different.

Rather than choosing an animal that equates to your best game, your
dream game and your key words, I'd like you to pick your favourite
player. It has to be someone you aspire to be, no matter how unrealistic
that is.

Of course, it's vital that this player competes in the same role as you on
the pitch. There's no point in choosing Lionel Messi if you're a
goalkeeper. If you tend to play in a couple of positions then by all
means pick two players.

Now add one or two key words to your model player. Here are some
examples:

- Confident Gerrard
- Focused, athletic Hamm
- Relaxed, calm Ronaldo
- Positive, upbeat Hart

There are so many examples to choose from. You'll know who is right
for you. Like the animal, the player must excite you and tease the best
from your body.

Whether you choose an animal or role model to attach to your key words is entirely up to you – there is no right or wrong. It is dependent on what is more meaningful to you. Here are some examples:

Goalkeeper

Brave Confident Hart

1. Jump with strength
2. Be loud – command back line
3. Act with confidence

Defender

Confident Lion

1. Head up – know where defenders are
2. Play on toes – confident at all times
3. Strong challenges – let strikers know I'm there

Midfielder

Clear Relentless Gerrard

1. Box to box – always impactful
2. Squeeze team up quickly
3. Close space with speed

Winger

Brave Lively Cheetah

1. Take on full backs
2. Stay positive no matter what
3. Always make an impact

Striker

Dominant Greyhound

1. Relentless movement to find space
2. Defend from the front
3. Attack the six yards

Some players like to simplify their script down to their key words, animals and models – others don't. It's about personal preference.

The advantage of doing so is that the main body of your script can be encompassed in two or three words. So if you take the striker example above, moving relentlessly and defending from the front can easily be aligned with being a dominant greyhound on the pitch. So can attacking the six-yard area. A predatory greyhound attacks its victim – it attacks the six yards. That's an incredibly powerful image to place in your mind going into a game.

"I'm a dominant greyhound. That is who I am and that is what I do. I'm relentless with my movement to find space and I work hard to defend from the front. I'm non-stop. I'm constantly striving to attack the six-yard area to give myself a great chance to score. I'm a dominant greyhound. That is what I do and that is who I am."

Whether you choose to use your key words, the animal technique, or your role model is of less importance to me. Of significance is that you have a script that relates to things that you can control, that will help you get the very most from your performance as an individual and a team mate, and which help give you the best possible chance of the best possible outcome.

Your goal for a game of soccer is to go and execute your script – performance and outcome will take care of themselves.

A Script for an Oscar

So what is your script? What plays can you include in this man of the match tool?

I want you take your time thinking about your script before writing it down. When you've completed it, make sure it's accessible to you daily. Much of this section will teach you what to do with your script in the days leading up to a game – needless to say I don't want you to write it out then put it in a drawer somewhere. I want it visible, so write it out again and again, and put it in several different locations. Make it a screen saver on your phone.

Be relentless with your script. Make it an everyday thing, an every week thing, an every month thing. Put it at the centre of your footballing world.

With no script you will have no structure for your mindset on the pitch. It's not only a great preparation tool it's also an important strategy to use to help you play with certainty and with focus. Its content will help you deal with the toughest of distractions.

If there were Oscars given out for soccer scripts I want yours to be a nominee for the top prize. A great script helps you become a great actor on the pitch, and as I will now discuss in the next two chapters, you need mental tools to help your script function at its very best.

Technique Number 8

Your goal for a game of soccer is to go and execute your script – performance and outcome will take care of themselves

9

Your First Controller

Filling your energy and confidence bars, as well as developing an intelligent and role specific match script, are your first steps in preparing to perform under pressure.

Now I'd like to teach you the mechanics behind executing your script, managing your energy and maintaining your confidence as you compete. I want to teach you this, in the preparation section of the book rather than the performance section, because I believe footballers must know precisely, in detail, what they have to do when they step onto the pitch.

You need to know the exact psychological mechanisms that will prevent your energy bars getting too low. You need to know the precise mental techniques that will help you retain confidence, irrespective of all the negatives that can confront you when you compete. And, given that you now have an awesome match script with plays resembling your responsibilities, key words, animal and role model, you need to know what mental tactics you can employ to perform your script.

To do this, I'm going to break the most powerful mind management techniques down into their simplest forms. I think there is nothing more important in sport psychology than keeping things straightforward. It makes it easier for you to take control consistently, at the vital moments, under pressure. Allow me to introduce you to your controllers.

Your Controllers

If you love soccer, I could take an educated guess that you've played one of the FIFA games on Xbox or PlayStation. In fact, I don't think

I've ever worked with a footballer who, despite being featured on the game, didn't love whiling away a few hours playing FIFA.

It's always funny working with a Premier League player who chooses to play for Barcelona or Real Madrid on FIFA. It happens to be even funnier when I watch a client be themselves in the game – quite often I joke with them that our goal is to get them as good in real life as they are when they play themselves on FIFA.

I'm not much of a gamer myself but I can see the attraction. Step into the world of Rory McIlroy, or a U.S. Marine, or an all action hero ready to take on an alien nation invading earth, and let your imagination run wild. Some of the mental side of soccer is related to using your imagination, and I see the fun in exercising this mental muscle whilst getting lost in another world. The ability to take control of a sporting icon, a super human, or a figure from a planet far, far away can be liberating and invigorating.

And the emphasis must be on the word *control*. Gaming is about taking *control* of someone else or something else and guiding that character through the trials and challenges that are thrown at them. To reach the end unscathed, or to win the trophy, your control has to be precise – a wrong direction, an unsure move, or a mistimed motion can send you back to the beginning or can hand the tournament to another victor.

Control in the world of gaming has changed over the years. For me, as a teenager, it used to be directed by a joystick. Today it's through a controller. It's no longer a clumsy 'stick' with an over-sized button. It's sleek. It's designed for speed. It's designed for dexterity. It's designed for hand, fingers and brain to work in harmony for real time control.

Your soccer mindset controllers are similar. They are built for speed. They can be applied in the moment. They are built for dexterity. They can be used in any footballing environment, on any pitch, in any country. They have followed you your whole life and you use them consciously and subconsciously every minute of every day. You carry them with you, always.

You have two controllers that you can use to execute and manage your energy and confidence bars as well as your match script. They are your body language and your self-talk. You can use them to help you perform to the best of your abilities on the pitch consistently, and under pressure.

"My two controllers are my body language and my self-talk. They help me retain energy, play with confidence and execute my script"

I want you to read this and repeat this.

"My two controllers are my body language and my self-talk. They help me retain energy, play with confidence and execute my script"

I want you to memorise it. Your body language and your self-talk are the controllers that will retain your energy, sustain your confidence and will help you achieve an 'Oscar' winning match script.

Let's start with your body controller by introducing you to a couple of American psychology researchers who are helping show the world how to optimise performance.

Your Body Controller

They possibly don't know it, but Dana Carney of British Colombia University and Amy Cuddy an associate professor at Harvard University are a *big* deal in the football world. In fact, whilst I would guess that the majority of players and coaches have never heard of these two brilliant academics, if players took heed of what they have discovered, and if coaches incorporated their work into training sessions, there would be a great deal more mental toughness enjoyed in the competitive world of football.

Carney and Cuddy have worked together on pioneering studies into nonverbal behaviour, hormonal change and performance. The premise of their work over the last few years has been simple, they have tried to bring scientific credibility to the old and worn idea that body language makes a difference to how we feel and subsequently impacts how we perform. Their findings are dramatic, illuminating and should have an impact on every soccer player.

Power Poses

In their research, Carney and Cuddy placed participants in a number of poses they labelled as 'power poses'. To give you an idea of what they looked like, one was called 'The Superman' (envision Superman, hands on hips, standing as tall as possible, chest pushed out – I think you get the picture!) Essentially, they were asking people to fake dominance and to fake power.

Experimental participants were asked to hold these power poses for a couple of minutes and then the two scientists measured any hormonal changes that might have taken place over this short period. They discovered that by simply placing people into these powerful positions, participants had an increase in testosterone levels and a decrease in the stress hormone, cortisol. Notably, the power poses also increased the participants' appetite for taking risk. Carney and Cuddy demonstrated that our bodies can change how we think and how we feel through hormonal change. Our bodies can change our minds.

Even more revealing was their efforts to show that a change of body language and subsequent hormonal shift can make a difference to performance. They had suspected that it was in pressure situations – times where people feel they are being judged, such as interviews and presentations, where a difference would be seen most graphically. So they set about testing their theory and indeed found that those who went through a process of power poses before a job interview were more successful during the interview process than those who were asked to portray low status poses before an interview (such as slumping the body). Amy Cuddy claimed that the difference between the two groups (low status and power pose) was that the power pose interviewees showed greater presence. They spoke passionately and confidently and they were more captivating and looked more comfortable.

What Carney and Cuddy have done through their use of scientific research is to demonstrate that using your body language can alter outcomes. They are careful to explain that whilst their project might have started out as a 'fake it to make it' study, results made clear that the term 'fake' wasn't accurate. They now describe the intentional use of body language as 'be it to become it'.

In short, act powerfully, think powerfully and develop the potential to perform powerfully.

The Mind Body Link

So what does all this mean to your game of soccer? Let me be clear. I don't think walking around like superman is going to help you become Lionel Messi. But, taking control of how you hold yourself, how you walk and how you project yourself helps you take control of your match script. It helps you manage your energy and confidence bars.

I call this mind body link your *body controller*. It enables you to turn up the volume of the most crucial mental qualities you need to play at your best. It helps you emphasise confidence and focus as you warm up. It helps you deal with the challenges the game delivers as you fight for possession, as you move to get on the ball, as you stalk the opposition's goal and as you defend your own penalty area.

Your body controller emphasises an important two way process – where mind meets body and body meets mind. As much as your psychology affects the functioning of your body, so how you hold your body also affects your brain. This is something scientists call a *positive feedback loop*.

I want all my clients to take ownership of the loop between their mind and body. I want all my clients to use their body controller for every second of every game. I want you to use this loop to help you execute your script.

I want you to warm up using your body controller. I want you to act out your match script using your controllers. I want you to act with confidence to maintain confidence. If it requires being on your toes then intentionally get on your toes. If it requires you to be sharp then be sharp. Be it to become it.

Be it to become it. Be sharp to become sharp. Be lively to become lively. Be upbeat to become upbeat.

On the pitch, your body controller consists of four functions or buttons:

- Your head (head up, always looking, always taking information in, vocal at the right times, looking alert, acting focused)
- Your shoulders (holding yourself tall, in a ready position)
- Knees (a powerful kick, a strong run, an aggressive challenge)
- Toes (staying alert by being on your toes, executing skills)

How do you hold yourself on the pitch? What do others see when you go a goal up? What do they see when you go a goal down?

What actions do you take? Do you close down the opposition with commitment and aggression? Do you clip the ball confidently to team mates?

How do you hold yourself and what actions do you take? Are you constantly head, shoulders, knees and toes? Are you relentless with your body controller?

The body controller is incredibly powerful. I've worked with players who have struggled with maintaining their focus. They tended to become disengaged from the game. They tended to switch off. I've asked them to re-engage by using their body controller, specifically by using their head. I asked them to play head up at all times, wide eyed, and to be constantly vocal. Accompanied with the second controller (which I'm going to introduce to you to in the next chapter) this offered a perfect recipe for staying switched on and dealing with distractions.

I've worked with Premier League strikers who have approached me because they have experienced a barren spell of goals. Simply by asking them to act ready at all times and act sharp with their toes they have found space easier and subsequently started to score. Simply by engaging their body controller to execute their match script they've got back to that winning feeling of scoring goals.

The key to your body controller's effectiveness is the level of belief you place behind it. I've found that players who buy into this notion of body influencing mind run onto the pitch knowing that they can manage themselves – they can influence their energy levels, their confidence and the plays in their script.

That is an incredibly liberating feeling to have:

"I have filled my bars, I now just have to use my body controller to manage their levels. If I start to lose energy I'll ignore any lethargy, I'll get on my toes and play with commitment and an unrelenting pace. If I lose confidence, I will play head up. I will be vocal. I will hold myself tall."

Your bars are full and you can use your body controller – your head, shoulders, knees and toes to keep them topped up. What does this look like? What does this feel like? When, during a game, might you have to do this? You can also use your body controller to nail your match script:

"My first play is to be aware of space. I will focus on that and will intentionally play head up and check both shoulders to get information around me – I will then act quickly on that information.

My second play is to constantly move. I will focus on that and will deliberately act it out – I will move non-stop using my knees and toes.

My third play is to jump high, with timing to win headers. I will focus on that and will out-jump the opposition by engaging my body controller at all times. I will keep my eye on the ball, be on my toes, and time my powerful jump perfectly."

Controlling your Script

You can choose to use the functions on your body controller at any time, no matter whether you are a goal up or a goal down. No matter the opposition, no matter the pitch you are playing on, no matter the weather, no matter the quality of the training sessions you have had, no matter who your coach is, no matter who is watching.

If you go a goal down, engage your body controller to maintain energy and confidence and to stay focused on your script. Do so if you make a mistake, if the referee is making dodgy decisions, if the opposition is playing well, if you're losing a personal battle, if your team mates are playing poorly, and if the crowd are getting on your back.

Keep your body controller engaged. And then double its effectiveness by getting your self-talk controller involved as well. Let's now talk more about that.

Technique Number 9

Use your body controller at all times to keep your
bars filled and to execute your match script.

10

Your Second Controller

Since deciding to specialise as a football psychologist, I have always watched soccer in a different way to others. Fans, coaches and players will watch a game and take in the external – the rolling of the ball, the movement of the teams, the momentum of play from one half to another.

I take all of those things into consideration when I'm watching a soccer match too, but primarily I'm focused on the internal that is driving the external. I'm considering the thoughts the players are experiencing. I'm reflecting on the feeling and emotions that are coursing through their veins.

Of course, as discussed in the last chapter, I'm watching for body language as well. I'm watching for player movement and activity – do they look sharp, lively and alert, or do they seem lethargic, tense and tight?

Body language is a revealing window into what a player is thinking and feeling. A footballer who is hiding and not showing for the ball suggests an inner doubt or worry. A soccer player who has gone quiet implies stress or anxiety. So I look long and hard for tell-tale signs of inner turmoil – if you look closely you really can see this on the outside.

I believe that your education as a footballer is incomplete without an appreciation of the internal that drives the external. And to become exceptional at controller number two you really do have to commit to becoming more aware of your inner world. That is where you second controller lives.

The Talk of a Champion

Your second controller is the voice you carry with you as you compete. It's that inner speech that never leaves your side. It's your self-talk.

If you want to play at your best under pressure – use your self-talk. If you want to compete hard, with confidence – use your self talk. If you want to sustain your energy in that last lung busting 10 minutes – use your self-talk. If you want to calm yourself down after a bad challenge from the opposition or following a refereeing decision you disagree with – use your self-talk. If you want to carry out your match script with relentless intensity – use your self-talk.

Your self-talk is a series of words, sentences and phrases that remain private to you, but which guide you through your everyday life. It's that inner voice that sends you left or right. It's the one that tells you to stop or to go. It's that dialogue that works somewhere between thinking and doing and helps you act on the decisions you mentally make. Your self-talk controller is the perfect accompaniment to your body controller – together they are a powerful antidote to inner turmoil and outer failure.

A famous psychologist once said, "Stop listening to yourself and start talking to yourself". This is an important sentence that should permeate throughout the global soccer community. Rather than being a slave to the errant thoughts that can destroy your focus and your confidence – the ones that can fire doubt through your mind and body – ensure that you answer all destructive thoughts with strong, upbeat and confident self-talk.

Self-talk can supply you with inner belief. You can use it to remind yourself of you at your best. You can use it as you warm up – as a prompt to focus, to get on your toes, to make an impact and to play free. You can use it to give yourself a motivational pep talk when it's needed most. When you're distracted you can remind yourself of the task at hand, specifically your match script. You can use it as a pick-me-up and you can urge yourself to remain upbeat and energised irrespective of score or mistake.

I want you to imagine this now. A vital match – one you've been waiting for. Perhaps a crunch league fixture or an exciting semi-final cup tie. It's 0-0 going into the final ten minutes when you fall behind to a sloppily conceded goal. What do you say to yourself now? What do you tell your body to do? What do you say to keep your energy and confidence bars at their maximum?

When I work with competitors from all sports, I help them use self-talk to work harder through the final 10 minutes. Athletes will use their inner voice to drive them on through pain, through wind and cold and rain and heat. Baseball players will demand better from themselves if they throw waywardly or strike out. Boxers will whisper strategic reminders to their bodies – the ones they need to use as their fights play out. Tennis players will scream with delight as they win a point that may have seemed lost during an endless rally – but they will also quietly remind themselves to stay cool and calm as the match progresses.

Excellence in football isn't just found amongst dancing feet. Excellence is also created within the quiet corridors of the mind.

- *Your self-talk sustains your energy – talk to yourself about maintaining hard work on the pitch*
- *Your self-talk retains your confidence levels – talk to yourself about looking confident, acting confident and displaying a confident attitude*
- *Your self-talk helps you stick like super glue to your match script – talk to yourself constantly about executing your script. Remind yourself relentlessly.*

Your Thinking and Your Self-Talk

There is a difference between your thinking and your self-talk. Your thoughts happen to you, you *do* your self-talk.

Let me write that again because I really want you to understand the very subtle difference. Your thoughts happen to you, you *do* your self-talk. Allow me to furnish you with an example to make myself clear about what I mean:

You're walking down the street and pass an Indian restaurant. The delicious curry smell hits you and something automatically pops into your head, "What shall I have for dinner tonight?" That's a thought. You engage your mind and tell yourself "I've got a couple of choices – chicken or fish." That's your self-talk. Your thoughts happen to you; you *do* your self-talk. Let me give you another example:

You are walking down the street with a friend when something pops into your head… "It's my sister's birthday tomorrow and I've forgotten to get her a gift." That's a thought. It's just randomly popped into your head, into your consciousness. You then engage your mind and tell yourself, "Okay I've got time this afternoon, I'll pop down to the mall and get her a present." That's your self-talk. Your thoughts happen to you, you *do* your self-talk.

I find it really useful to differentiate between thoughts and self-talk when talking with clients about the power of the second controller. I want them to understand, that the self-talk controller is (as its name suggests) a controller. You can use it to take control of yourself in any given situation.

I'm sure you've already realised by now that self-talk is an important life skill as much as it is a vital soccer skill. Becoming accomplished at using your self-talk can help you problem solve and find solutions in many challenging situations. The greatest entrepreneurs are the ones who engage their self-talk during tough times. They become 'can do' when others would say 'can't'.

The same can be said of elite sports competitors. The Olympians who bring home the gold medals are the ones who have great self-talk to accompany the skill in their hands or legs. The best tennis players talk their way through the pressure points in a Grand Slam tournament. The greatest golfers talk their way through 18 pressure-filled holes to post the lowest scores of the day.

I want this for you. I want you to be outstanding with your self-talk. I want you to drive the skills you have in your feet through the natural audio system you have in your mind.

Your Inner Audio Player

- *"Keep working – stick to my script"*
- *"On my toes - lively, lively, lively"*
- *"I feel so tired – keep working though, great body language – keep my energy bar high"*
- *"Oh no, a goal already – let's stay focused, remind everyone to keep great body language and stick to my script"*
- *"This girl is quick and strong – stick to the script, stay with the script"*

If I was to install an inner audio player that tracked what you say to yourself what would I hear? Would I hear helpful, constructive and positive self-talk? Would I hear you energising yourself? Would I hear you striving to keep your confidence bar high? Would I hear a lot of talk about your script?

Or would I hear thoughts that are unhelpful, destructive and negative? Would I hear thoughts and self-talk that de-energise you? Would I hear thoughts and self-talk that can reduce your confidence? And would I fail to hear self-talk about your script that can keep you focused, on track, and bang on the responsibilities within your role?

I'm going to talk more about negative thoughts in the next section of the book, but for now I want you to imagine that your coach is recording all the vocal inputs that pass through your mind. I want you to strive to help your coach hear the kind of self-talk that your greatest fan would inject into your mind. I want you to keep that audio trail energetic, confident and related to the script.

A Controller Combo

What could be more powerful than using your two controllers on the pitch to be the very best you can be? That amazing combination can sustain your energy and confidence bars as well as focus your mind to execute your script.

I have written about your controllers in the preparation section of this book because I want you to prepare to play by practicing them in training. Make them an important part of your individual development programme. Include them in your training script.

Keeping incredible body language and confident self-talk are merely two skills that anyone can improve. You don't have to have the deft touch of a Lionel Messi or the vision of a Ronaldo to be world class at managing your body language and keeping effective self-talk.

But despite their simplicity, the impact of getting them right can be profound. I've helped young players in England, France and Spain break into their professional first teams by engaging their controllers. I've helped League 2 players move up one or two divisions just by introducing them to their controllers. I've helped seasoned footballers make their International debuts by getting them to take control of their body and self-talk.

They work. Start practicing them. Believe in them. Be ready to take them onto the pitch with you. But before you do let's power up their batteries.

Technique Number 10

Use your self-talk, in combination with your body controller, to keep your energy and confidence bars high and to focus on your script.

11

Your Inner Batteries

Working with me is demanding. When a soccer player (professional or recreational) contacts me to help them improve their game I'm quite clear with my words – I'm going to challenge you.

I'm going to try to squeeze the most out of you that I can. If you want to get better than you ever thought you could be, then you're going to have to let me be ruthless with you. Average is unacceptable in my world, only your best will do.

Everything we talk about, and everything I ask you to do, will be simple. But there's a difference between simple and easy – straightforward still requires willpower and discipline. You'll be stretched. You'll be asked to deliver comfort zone busting attitudes and behaviours.

When a player contacts me, I'm also very aware that they will have an opinion about sport psychology. Perhaps they've been told by a coach that it's only for players with problems. Or perhaps they've had a team mate who found seeing a sport psychologist unhelpful.

I ask all new clients to keep an open mind about the tools and techniques we'll be working on. As you will have already discovered from reading the opening chapters in this book (and from my other soccer books) I'm not a big fan of psychology that can be seen as too funky or weird. I like to keep things straightforward. My clients and I don't put our thumbs and forefingers together and chant, I've never suggested a footballer should go and hug a tree, and I've never asked a soccer team to start howling at the moon. But I do require players to be honest at all times, and I do need them to be open to exploring and understanding how their brains and minds function.

I say this to you because sometimes work on your psychology requires a little bit of a leap of faith. Improving the mind cannot always be seen. We can view the consequences of the thoughts of a footballer (through body language and other external tell-tale signs) but as yet we can't reliably measure the mind and its impact on performance. Players can tell me they've played well or feel more confident with their game, but these alone aren't proof that psychology is a tool for improvement.

If I was to start working with you, I would be honest about this. We'd discuss what you do and do not know about the brain and mind and their relationship with soccer. I would likely tell you that some of the philosophies we talk about and several of the techniques we strive to apply may require you to slip into a 'believing' mentality. You may not be able to completely see it work, but you have to trust that what you are doing *will* work and *is* working.

There is one such technique that I want to introduce to you now. It will form a vital part of your preparation. It can't be seen by others but it *can* have a profound effect on your energy and confidence bars, the execution of your match script, and how effectively you use your two controllers.

Your Inner Movie

In Soccer Tough, I dedicated a whole chapter to the art of using your imagination. I like players to spend at least five minutes a day (preferably up to 15 minutes) preparing for an upcoming fixture by taking some quiet time to picture the game they'd like to play. I like them to create a detailed blueprint of their future performance in their mind, readying themselves for the pressure moments ahead.

You may have heard of terms like visualisation, imagery or mental rehearsal. These words refer to the process of using the pictures you experience in your mind to help you develop skills and aid your readiness to perform. Personally, I try to avoid words such as visualisation as I prefer to keep things simple. I ask my players to 'picture' their performance – that is all.

All great athletes, all great champions, picture events before they play and perform. The internal images that flash up before their mind's eye provide them with a sense of readiness and a sense of certainty and assurance.

What will it look like if you play at your very best in your next game? What will it feel like? What will others see?

Interestingly, picturing your upcoming game does more than provide you with a psychological security blanket. Scientists have found that the brain and nervous system can't tell the difference between what's real and what's imagined. When you take the time to picture yourself playing – by using your imagination to play out different scenarios on the pitch before they have actually happened – the brain actually thinks that you are competing. And this process can build the kind of race tracks in your mind that I spoke about in the first section of this book.

Of course, it's important to rationalise how much impact picturing can have on your game. It isn't a replacement for physical practice – I would never say that to a player. So, let's not blow things out of proportion. Picturing holding aloft a trophy or 'seeing' a positive score-line won't make this actually happen, unfortunately. But creating inner images and movies of your picture perfect game for an upcoming match is a really useful technique to engage in. And there are several ways to optimise your picture creation time – to make them relevant and impactful.

Picture Perfect

So what should you picture for five to fifteen minutes a day? What inner pictures will help clear your mind of clutter and focus your attention with efficiency?

Allow me to suggest the three components of preparation and performance that you should be picturing:

1. Your energy and confidence bars
2. Your match script
3. Your controllers

I will take you through each component one by one.

Build your Bars

What does it look like when you play with a full *energy* bar? What does it feel like?

- Energy – non stop and relentless. A full bar – making runs, movement, on your toes – always looking, always thinking what next?
- The energy to fill the space, to close down, to sprint when jogging would be satisfactory
- Wide eyed, ready at all times – watching – the runs of the opposition, the movement of your team mates

What does conserving energy look like? Feel like? When do you conserve your energy? How many sprints will you need to make?

What does it look like when you play with a full *confidence* bar? What does it feel like?

- Confidence – holding yourself proud, clipping crisp crosses into the box, driving with the ball
- Carrying on no matter what, in spite of a mistake, in spite of going a goal down

What does a full confidence bar look like? Feel like? What does a full energy bar look like, feel like?

Make your images big and bold and bright. Push your feelings of confidence and energy through your body from head to toe. Incredible confidence, Incredible energy. What does this look like? What does this feel like?

Load your Script

Football is a performance – what does your finest performance look like? Feel like? What would others see? What would they say?

You have a script with a number of plays. These are your goals – a great game is dependent on you executing them with energy and confidence. What does this look like and feel like?

Make your images big and bold and bright. Picture playing your script through your own eyes and from the side of the pitch. Picture perfect – what do you see, feel and hear?

Imagine yourself in the changing room before the game, ready. Whether you are quiet or loud, picture what you normally do, what you like to do. Imagine yourself in that room with confidence flowing through you. Imagine yourself looking at your script, thinking about your script. Imagine those final few moments before you go play – looking composed, looking assured, looking eager to compete.

"I am bang on my script every second of every game – from warm up to the final whistle. I focus. I deal with distraction with speed by getting back to my script immediately. There is no hesitation on the pitch. There is only my script, there are only the responsibilities within my role."

Make your inner pictures big and bold and bright. Light up excellence in your mind with an intense dazzling display of you playing at your best. Burn this into your mind. Staple it to your brain.

"When I compete, I am my script. I stick to it like super glue. I execute it with focus, with freedom and with fire. My script is who I am as a soccer player. My script is what I do no matter the game, no matter the opposition, no matter the conditions. I do not waver from my script. I am my script as a footballer. My script is me"

Power up Your Controllers

"I feel secure on the pitch. I feel at home. I have my two controllers – my self-talk and my body language."

What does it look like when I use them? What does it feel like?

Use your controllers with speed. Just like when playing a computer game such Fifa or Call of Duty, use your controllers with maximum speed and with complete precision.

When you need to turn up the volume of your self-talk, do so at will. When you need to instruct yourself about your script or your energy bars do so with an inner voice that shouts loudly – that commands and demands. Because that's what champions do in sport – they demand more from themselves as the game progresses.

You should now be starting to have incredible confidence and belief in yourself because you now know you can take complete control of yourself on the pitch. And you now know how to. Your self-talk and your body language are your twin management tools that prevent you from feeling lethargic or despondent. They can help you deal with fear and doubt and worry and anxiety. Employing them helps you regulate your emotions, helps your squash unwanted distractions, and helps you pay attention to the important cues on the pitch as the game progresses.

Imagine using your controllers constantly throughout the game. It's so simple, there are only two of them. Picture using your self-talk to keep your energy and confidence bars raised. Visualise using your controllers to maintain your concentration on your match script.

"I feel in complete control when I play. If I make a mistake, I use my controllers. If we go a goal down I use my controllers. If I start to feel unhelpful emotions, I have an instant solution – my controllers…"

Picture Creation

Creating inner pictures that are personal to your soccer gives you a better chance of success in a match. Making your personal images rich with vivid pictures related to the things you can actually control heightens your sense of readiness for the game ahead. Imagery and visualisation can have a profound impact on your game provided you use your inner pictures in a very personal way and in a very specific way.

Create a private performance, away from the crowds, away from public attention. Watch yourself play everyday – watch and watch and watch. Mentally rehearse your script and use your controllers. It's like having a portable battery charger – you charge the batteries of your bars, your script and your controllers. Start to charge these on Monday, ready for a Saturday match. Re-charge daily – Tuesday, Wednesday, Thursday, and Friday. Put them on charge for 5-15 minutes daily. Be committed to this procedure. We're almost ready to play…

Technique Number 11

Charge your Inner Batteries Daily.

12

How Marley is learning to Mentally Contrast

Marley Watkins sighs down the phone – he's heard my question before.

"I'm going to stick to my script no matter what," he says, in subtle Welsh tones. "I'm going to stick to my script like glue. If I'm not getting on the ball then I'll make sure I'm on my controllers. I'll shout my script to myself and I'll keep great body language."

I understand his fatigue – I ask him the same thing every week and he responds with the same answers week in, week out. It's the habit I've tried to build into our relationship – the habit that will help him become the very best he can be.

The current Barnsley FC winger keeps talking, "If I make a mistake I'll use my self-talk and my body controller. I know my body language is so important, I have to keep on my toes. The full-back is a good one – really good positioning and he makes it hard for a winger to play a good final ball. I have to stay aggressive in everything I do, no let up."

As he speaks, I can hear the Barnsley winger's mind churning away. He's picturing what he's saying. He's mentally seeing his challenges and the problems he's going to face.

"If the referee makes a bad decision what are you going to do?" I ask. "What if you're not getting on the ball? If your team mates are having a poor game how are you going to react? What if you miss a great opportunity to score?"

My questions dial in to the kind of mentality I want him to display on the pitch. I'm hard on Marley. I'm tough because I care and because I want him to excel in every game. He can't play his best game all the time, but there is no reason why he shouldn't have his bars, his controllers, and his script locked and loaded for the match ahead.

The questions I ask him might seem strange to you, perhaps a little negative. But I'm asking Marley these kinds of questions on purpose. I want Marley to think flexibly about the upcoming game – I want him to be able to mentally contrast.

A Different Way of Thinking

It does make me chuckle when I hear a player tell me that they don't need to speak to me because they 'think positively' already. It makes me smile because the perception they have (that I'm a 'positive thinking guru') couldn't be further from the truth.

As you've already read in section one of this book, I help players to be able to think flexibly about their game. I teach them to maintain confidence while at the same time being able to look unemotionally at the cold hard facts of their game. They aren't going to improve if they don't study their weaknesses.

To all those players who believe that sport psychology is about 'positive thinking' I'm here to tell you that you're wrong. Sport psychology teaches the discipline of thinking flexibly. Sport psychology helps you learn how to think in a robust, practical way.

It may surprise you to hear that I don't want you to limit your thinking going into a match. I don't want you to solely direct your thoughts towards the positive. Sure, I *do* want you to envision playing at your very best. And of course I think it's essential to picture perform your script with perfection. But the very best preparation encompasses a vital look at what you'll do when it goes wrong.

This is something a very influential psychologist called Gabrielle Oettingen has researched for many years. She calls it mental contrasting.

She argues that to give yourself the very best possible chance to achieve the goals you set yourself in life you have to spend a little time thinking about what can go wrong. You have to spend a little time focusing on the obstacles that can prevent you from achieving your goal.

So, for example, if someone has a goal of getting fit they should think about the obstacles that stand between them and being fit. Examples include being too tired to go to the gym or being invited out to eat by friends. Oettingen argues that to give yourself the best possible chance of reaching your goal of getting fit, you need to have strategies to deal with these obstacles. In the case of our examples above, you might choose to have a few pieces of gym equipment at home so if you don't feel like heading out to the gym you can do things in the comfort of your living room. If you've been invited to a meal out, you might choose to have a salad rather than anything too fatty (no matter how tough that can be!).

So why is all of this relevant to you the soccer player? Well every game of football will present obstacles and tests that can prevent you from executing your script and playing to your very best ability. Think about what some of them might be. Poor refereeing decisions, the great play of the opposition, a terrible set of performances from your team mates, horrible weather, and a poor pitch are a few that you might consider.

What are you going to do if any of the above happens? How are you going to react and respond? What's your next move? How can you keep your confidence and energy bars high? What will it look like if you employ your controllers with speed?

Brainstorming how you'll deal with the problems and challenges you'll face on the pitch is a detail you can't ignore if you want to be soccer tough. It's a five-minute mental procedure that separates champions from the runners up.

What Am I Going To Do?

When Marley Watkins is preparing to play, he opens his mind to what might happen. He knows that games of football don't always go according to plan. He knows that he's human and his body won't always feel attuned to excellence. He knows he has to battle hard to stay focused, confident and in control. Because of this, he commits himself every week to the process of mental contrasting:

- I might have a few bad touches in warm up – what am I going to do?
- I might give the ball away early in the game – what am I going to do?
- My midfield might struggle to get the ball to me – what am I going to do?
- My first cross might go into row Z – what am I going to do?
- I might miss a glorious chance to score – what am I going to do?

By asking himself "What am I going to do" he's creating a blueprint in his mind that he can carry into the game with him.

"I'm going to be relentless on my controllers. I'm going to be quick, speedy on my body controller and I'm going to be ruthless with my self-talk."

You see, Marley Watkins isn't going to have a perfect game every match. He's not even going to have a great game every match. But he's going to give himself a great opportunity to shine by taking the time to imagine the struggles and exertions he'll experience during his upcoming games. The cocktail of armchair solutions he blends in his mind will help him be the very best he can be on matchday. They'll help him be an uncompromising, tough and brutal competitor.

A Brutal Competitor

In the week leading up to the 2015 Scottish FA Cup Final, Marley and I had been talking about being a brutal competitor. It was, after all, the biggest game of his career.

Before Marley arrived at Barnsley to play in the English League Division One, he had played for Inverness in the Scottish Premier

League. During the 2014/15 season he had been one of the standout players and had been rewarded with a cup final appearance against Scottish club Falkirk.

Marley told me over the phone, a few days before the game, that he wanted to make a big impact. He wanted to cap an outstanding season by scoring and being the man of the match. I was quick to respond and get him focusing on the things he could control:

"What are the things that are going to stop you playing well? What will stop you being the best player on the pitch?"

Marley had a little think and then responded, "I know the defenders are going to be really up for it. They are strong and they're going to get tight to me. I'm not going to have much space or much room."

"Okay, so what are you going to do to combat that, Marley?" I asked him.

"I'm going to work all week on my movement – in this game I've got to be a step ahead and I've got to play with more energy than ever. I've got to keep my self-talk real strong and make sure I'm on my toes at all times. If we go a goal down I can't give up – I have to have a relentless mindset."

I loved that answer, and I sent him a text message straight after our call to remind him of what he had said to me. I asked him to look at the message daily. I wanted him to see his own words every day leading into the game.

On the day of the game, Marley was ready. He had mentally contrasted during the week and he was prepared for anything the Falkirk defenders wanted to throw at him.

And so, when the game kicked off, Marley did what he had told me he was going to do. He was sharp and alive and athletic. He played head up and on his toes. Midway through the first half, his team mate found him with a through ball that split the defence open. Marley, playing with energy and confidence, got on the end of the pass and rounded the goalkeeper. He then gently caressed the ball into the back of the net.

As he ran off towards the corner flag in celebration, he let out a scream of delight. The dozens of conversations he had had on the phone with me about his mindset – about confidence and energy and focus and controllers and dealing with distractions – had all been worth it. He was discovering his own personal brand of excellence.

And that day will stick in the mind of Marley Watkins for the rest of his life. Inverness went on to claim the cup with Marley making an assist for the winning goal in the second half. He was crowned man of the match at the end of the game. He had been a brutal and brilliant competitor.

The Marley in You

This is what I want for you. I want you to be an uncompromising, tough and brutal competitor. I want you to do what Marley does – I want you to mentally contrast your matches before you go and play.

When 'stuff' happens on the pitch, I want your mind to be clear and nimble – not burdened by distraction. I want your brain beating with speed and attuned to solution. The past is over, the last second has gone – what next, what next?

And with the technique of mental contrasting a new firm favourite, you are ready to play. Your internal batteries are charged, your bars are filled, your controllers are ready to fire, your script has been written and you have solutions for every eventuality. Now you are prepared. Now you are ready to go be a great individual player and an incredible team mate. Now you are ready to go play soccer tough.

Technique 12

Picture the bad to come up with the good –
mentally contrast before every game.

Prepare Pep Talk

Too many soccer players leave confidence to chance. They aren't fussy about their confidence. They aren't purposeful with this most important of inner feelings. They can be similarly casual about their energy. They make assumptions. They presume they'll turn up to a game and feel full of energy.

Be intentional with your confidence. And be deliberate with your energy. Get to know exactly what actions, behaviours, attitudes, processes and thoughts help you prepare to play with confidence and energy.

Leave no stone left unturned. Like a detective, hunt down the clues that leave you crackling with confidence and find the evidence that helps electrify your energy.

Whatever you uncover, go to work on your confidence and on your energy bars everyday. Anxiety and lethargy are the alternatives, and they are not the fit of a champion footballer.

Raise your confidence and energy bars daily

*

I know you want to win. That's what the game is all about right? But what are you going *to do* to win? Soccer is a game that is driven by process, by actions and specific mental qualities that give a great performance and subsequent victory their strongest opportunity.

If you're a striker, I know you want to score. If you're a defender or goalkeeper, I know you want to keep a clean sheet. What are you going to *do* to achieve these outcomes? They are out of your control and it is your job to focus your mind on the things you *can* control.

I want you to write out a script and go and execute it. When you make a mistake come back to your script. When you find yourself thinking in an unhelpful way come back to your script. When you're reflecting on past plays or dwelling on things that didn't go the way you wanted them to go, shift back to your script.

That is mental toughness. That is intelligent soccer. That is controlled football.

Your goal for a game of soccer is to go and execute your script – performance and outcome will take care of themselves.

*

As much as your psychology affects your physiology, so your physiology affects your psychology.

Your body can be used for more than just swerving and heading, passing, shooting and tackling. It's equipped with the power to help you maintain confidence and energy. It's armed with the capability to help you stay focused and alert, ready to compete every second of every game.

Stand tall. Get on your toes. Dance your feet. Lift your head, open your eyes and look around you. These are functions of your body controller. Use them. Use them when your distraction scatters your concentration. Use them when you start to feel flat or despondent. Use them when your energy is sapping or when your confidence begins to ebb.

Use your body controller at all times to keep your bars filled and to execute your match script.

*

Your self-talk is different to your thinking. Your thoughts *happen* to you, you *do* your self-talk.

This is an important difference. Champions are accomplished at talking to themselves as they compete. Their self-talk lengthens their stride, sustains their drive and reminds them of what's important.

Combine your body controller with your self-talk controller. Say and do as you compete. Say and do, say and do, say and do...

Use your self-talk in combination with your body controller to keep your energy and confidence bars high and to focus on your script.

*

What you see can be what you get.

I want you to see powerful inner pictures of the football factors that you are in full control of. I want you to take a little time daily to see yourself competing with your energy and confidence bars crammed. I want you to picture playing your match script. And I want you to see yourself using your controllers on the pitch.

Charge your inner batteries. Create a mental blueprint for the things you can control. Power up your processes so that you let your performance take care of itself. In this way, you spray perfect and precise processes on your brain and nervous system.

See your script, feel your script. See your bars, feel your bars. See your controllers in action. Feel your controllers in action.

Charge your inner batteries daily

*

Prepare to be a brutal competitor on the pitch. Engage in mental contrasting.

Know exactly what it is you are going to do when it goes wrong. And it *will* go wrong. Shots will be missed and mistakes will be made. The weather will turn and the opposition will play some great soccer.

Irrespective of the level you play football at, things will go wrong. Brainstorm your solutions before you set foot on the pitch. Ask yourself what you are going to do in every given circumstance.

If you go a goal down, what are you going to do? If your team mates are playing poorly, what are you going to do? If you lose confidence, what are you going to do?

Be an intelligent footballer. Be a soccer player ready to take on the lows of the game. As the match unfolds, there will be plenty of challenging moments and you need to strategise *before* you play to be a brutal competitor *while* you play.

Picture the bad to come up with the good – mentally contrast before every game.

Perform – Introduction

You've been practicing your game, and you've been using your training script to improve your skills. You've laid down your match script, filled your bars, and charged your inner batteries. You have your controllers to hand and now you're ready to play. Now you're ready to compete.

This is the time the best – most meticulous – preparation can go wrong. Soccer players can get tense. They can become anxious the closer they get to kick off. Doubt and worry can creep up on them, fog their mind, choke their freedom and envelope their game in fear.

Relax… Stay calm… Be patient

I know you want to play well but you can't force your best game. You can't force greatness. What you *can* do is complete a series of tasks before you kick off that will optimise your body and mind for the game ahead.

This section starts by introducing you to the concept of a matchday mindset – a philosophy to compete by, and a set of habits filtered into a routine that you can execute as the match draws nearer.

Then we'll discuss your in-game mindset:

- How to deal with unhelpful, destructive thinking on the pitch… quickly!

- The advantage of playing with fun, freedom and focus

- What to think and when to do

- Performing confidently under pressure

The great players see an opening because their mind is open to that opening. A great defender has a mind that is aware of the space the striker might run into. The great midfielder has a mind that is aware of the space that he can exploit. The great striker has a mind that is aware of the space that she can score from. All these players have a mind that is clear and calm and unfogged by doubt and worry.

Stay calm… Relax… Be patient

All you can be is the very best you can be on the pitch. That is all. That is all you can ask from yourself. That is all you can demand from yourself. This section will give you some powerful philosophies and strategies to make that a reality.

13

A Matchday Mindset

Neymar was out injured and captain Thiago Silva had a match ban, but even the most apprehensive Brazilian supporter couldn't have predicted what was about to unfold in the Estadio Mineirao.

Tuesday 8th July 2014 – the World Cup semi-finals. Home turf for the most successful soccer nation in history with 200 million fans screaming their support across the country. The city of Belo Horizonte was bustling with yellow and green flags and optimism was high. For many, another final was inevitable – it had been their destiny ever since the country had been awarded the World Cup.

But the Brazilians were up against an in-form German team hungry to win the biggest prize in football. And the Brazilians had scraped and scrapped their way to the semi-finals with unconvincing performances delivered under the most intense pressure from their adoring fans. The Samba beats had been constant but the team had been average at best.

And what followed was a disaster for those who lined the beaches ready to celebrate another Brazilian win. It wasn't to be. Their beloved team was 5-0 down in less than 30 minutes – a ruthless, brutal German side capitalising on defensive mistake after mistake. Speed and mobility from the European team destroyed a Brazilian side that looked bereft of confidence, of focus, of self-belief.

Global fans watched in stunned disbelief. Experts on television were at a loss to explain the Brazilian implosion. Brazilian fans were simply swamped with grief. After the match, head coach of the beaten team – Luiz Felipe Scolari – announced it to be the worst day of his life, while Joachim Low, the German manager explained that Brazil had 'cracked up', meaning that they had folded under the intense pressure of the game.

A consolation goal from Oscar in the 90th minute left a scoreline of 7-1 to the dominant German team. The Brazilians, as Low described, had indeed cracked up. But such a folding under pressure is not unusual. It happens to players and teams week in, week out, the world over at every level of the game. Let's explore this phenomenon a little closer. By getting to know the roots of poor performance we can get to grips with high attainment.

Wonderful Doing Woeful

The happenings of that night in Belo Horizonte underpins one of the reasons why we love sport and watch sport. It's unpredictable. It throws up sensational stories of shock and upset, of underachievement and over-accomplishment.

That fateful semi-final for the Brazilian team was an example of the wonderful doing woeful. These were wonderful players performing woefully and fans, pundits and armchair experts across the footballing globe were shocked by what they saw – how could such a good team do so badly?

Allow me to give you my perspective of what happened to the Brazilian players that night – it will only take a few paragraphs.

How you behave and subsequently perform on the pitch is dominated by the hormones you release inside of you. Your inside drives your outside! That sounds weird but bear with me.

Think about a time when you laughed really hard and as a consequence felt very happy. That great feeling that bubbled inside your body was a result of hormones called endorphins being released.

Think about a time when you felt really competitive – when you were really up for a match or performance of some kind. That motivational feeling that surged through your body was a result of a hormone called testosterone.

Think about a time when you were really focused or engaged in an activity. That feeling of immersion happened because a hormone called dopamine was being injected into your body.

Think about a time when you felt very stressed, very anxious or tense. These feelings accompanied the release of cortisol, your stress hormone.

You see, quite simply, with every feeling you have, there is a hormone powering its way through your body that creates the feeling you experience. And these hormones are powerful. Once you start to release them, they not only determine your feelings, they also influence the behaviours you display and drive your performance.

It is vital that you learn how to release the hormones you need to feel good so you can perform as close to your best as you can. You've got to work on getting that winning feeling.

The Feeling of Winning

Science has demonstrated that as you start to perceive yourself as playing well, and as you start to believe you can win, your body begins to release a powerful combination of performance and feel good hormones. As success starts to hit you, a chemical called dopamine opens up the pleasure centre in your brain which in turn makes you feel great.

Then your performance hormones – testosterone and adrenaline – charge through your bloodstream giving you strength and alertness. You breathe deeper and provide the brain and your muscles with oxygen-rich blood. You experience a profound sense of wellbeing and you feel less tired and more euphoric.

When you're competing on the pitch this blend of performance and feel good hormones supercharge your mindset. You see more and you act quicker – your focus is sharper, and your reflexes are faster. You make better decisions. You feel like you have more time to act, to anticipate and to execute.

What does this look like? What does this feel like?

Look up and around – see the whole pitch. Feeling nimble and quick – see the space and run into it. Fill the danger area. Get the ball, give it back – lend it. See more and do more – be light on your toes.

What does a supercharged mindset look like? What does it feel like?

The German players had this feeling in abundance going into the match and when they went a couple of goals up inside the first 15 minutes their 'winning hormones' went into overdrive. They saw the gaps and spaces quicker, they were quick to react and first to the ball. They were stronger, more powerful and demonstrated greater athleticism than their rivals. The Brazilians by contrast had a different internal chemistry.

The Feeling of Losing

When you feel like you're starting to lose, you tend to enter a downward spiral. Dopamine and endorphins begin to dissipate causing the pleasure centres in your brain to start switching off. This losing feeling releases the stress hormone cortisol which, when mixed with the chemical adrenaline that is spreading throughout your body, leads you to feel anxious and fearful. You will experience a nasty sinking feeling and your body seizes up making coordinated movement tough to deliver. In drastic situations your body starts to become immobilised.

What does this look like? What does this feel like?

Tunnel vision – see less. Slow – lethargic movement. Sticky feet – turf feeling heavy. Weighed down – sluggish.

When the Brazilians lined up for the semi-final clash they were nervous, tense and fearful. They knew that only a win would do, but they were without their talismanic striker and without their leader. They knew that the Germans were strong – very strong. They knew that all of Brazil were hoping, if not praying, for a victory.

The combination of these three circumstances led to an enormous burden on the Brazilian team. The cortisol poured through the bloodstreams of those players causing a collective anxiety and a losing feeling that kicked in before they kicked off. Going a goal down early in the game only made this feeling worse.

The leaders in the team went quiet. Movement slowed and certain players started to hide. Defenders were unaware of their positions and of the runs the German players were making. The Germans were easily able to lose their markers and find space. The feeling of losing completely nullified the threat of the Brazilian footballers as an attacking force, and laid them open to conceding goals as a defensive unit.

And that was it –pretty much game over. Cortisol swamped the Brazilian players suppressing their game and diminishing their ability.

So how do you, the soccer player, ensure that this doesn't happen to you? How do you tap that winning feeling before you play?

Relaxation Marks the Spot

I'm going to surprise you a little here. I'm going to go against the grain of traditional pre-match thinking.

I believe you should never ever, ever try to force your performance. You are far better to relax completely – to take your mind away from the game entirely.

- *If you want to play at the right intensity, come kick off, then relax*
- *If you want to be energised, come kick off, then relax*
- *If you want to give yourself the best chance to play with confidence then relax*
- *If you want a clear mind, a mind ready to cope with the challenges the game throws at you, then relax*

Hear this and repeat this to yourself – you cannot force your performance. The more you try to, the worse it will get. The more you try to, the more stressed you will become. The more you try to, the tighter you will play.

I see it time and time again with players at every level. They play an important match and try that little bit too hard. It might be a youth team player competing in his first academy game. He wants to impress the coaching staff. He wants to show them how good he is. So he convinces himself that he needs to have his best ever performance. And he goes about trying to make that happen. Perhaps he runs around like a headless chicken, or perhaps he becomes so anxious about his game that he doesn't run at all. He becomes fearful and hides. He becomes scared and his movement is paralysed.

I see it at every level. I've seen it at the Women's World Cup. I've seen players wilt under the intense pressure of 'having to perform'. They get past the group stages and they think, "This is the most important match of my life, I have to be incredible today." They think, "I have to get this right otherwise I'll let everyone down – the coaching staff, my team mates, my family…" And so what happens? They play tight and tense and rigid. They play with a mind misted by confusion. They forget to use the mental mist wipers that they've used so effectively when playing for their club team back home. They are simply unable to play with a clear mind.

No one is immune to trying too hard. It is completely normal and understandable. And it is hard to fight against but it is imperative that you exercise your willpower to do so because forcing performance is one of the quietest, most ruthless killers in this game. It's killed FA Cup finalists. It's brutalised the games of Champions League players. Copa Del Rey matches have seen lower than expected performances from players who have taken to the pitch trying too hard to force their minds and bodies.

Maybe the Brazilian players who were so humbled during that fateful World Cup semi-final needed to relax more – not try so hard. Perhaps they needed to avoid a focus on the weight of expectation that had been placed upon them.

Instead, they possibly built themselves up into a frenzy. With their star player out injured, they strolled around with caps emblazoned with the words 'Forza Neymar' on them. Surely this heaped pressure upon pressure? Surely this created tension and stress and anxiety and worry amongst a collection of the best players in the world?

Relax... Stay calm... Remain quiet. Let's give ourselves a chance to raise our confidence and energy bars. Let's get our controllers ready for action. What does our best look like? What does our best feel like?

We can't force a great performance today. But we trust that when we stick to our scripts, and when we take complete control of ourselves using our self-talk controllers and our body controllers, then we'll be the very best we can be. And we can't do anymore.

Nobody can force their performance. Nobody can 'make it happen'. That's fantasy talk. That's not real life at the sharp end of soccer. I want all of my players to relax on the day of a game. I want them going in with a quiet mind and a body ready to deal with the stresses and strains of 90 minutes of fierce competition. That is why all my players have a matchday routine.

Make Your Routine, Routine

Every match must be treated in the same way. Every match must be approached in a similar manner. This is where a matchday routine comes in.

My first piece of advice about matchday is very, very important so please read carefully. I'm going to surprise you a little, but there's a very good scientific explanation behind what I'm about to offer.

From the moment you wake up I want you to avoid thinking about the game. I don't want you to think about it at all. I don't want you thinking about soccer until two hours before your kick off.

Why? Because you'll release your performance hormones far too early. You'll spill crucial stores of adrenaline.

Have you ever felt tired come kick off? Have you ever felt lethargic the moment the match begins? I've experienced an overwhelming *yes* to this question from countless players.

If you've found yourself feeling pretty exhausted before the match has begun, that's because you've been thinking too much about the game during the previous few hours. You've been picturing your performance time and again. This type of visualisation releases adrenaline too early and depletes your stores.

You see, as discussed in the previous section, the brain can't tell the difference between what's real and what's imagined. As you get that inner picture of how you want to play, so your brain thinks you are actually playing. And because the brain and nervous system thinks you're playing, they release adrenaline into your bloodstream. So your building blocks for performance diminish.

If you're a morning thinker – if you immerse yourself in your footballing world from the moment you wake – stop! Relax, chill and stay calm. Take your mind away from the game and your mind away from soccer in general. Conserve your energy bar!

Two Hour Countdown

Great soccer is a balance between relaxation and intensity. Now you are suitably relaxed in body and completely clear in mind it is time to start turning up the heat.

To do this, you have to get your match script out of your kit bag. It's time to start getting some incredible inner pictures of how you want to play – so have a read of your match script.

What does incredible with your script look like? Feel like?

What will others see if you execute your script with precision? What moves and actions will you make? How confident will you look?

As you play your script in your mind, make sure you send a flood of positive emotion through your body. Feel the force of freedom in your feet. Feel confidence ripple through your legs. Feel excitement swell in your belly. Let your physiology sizzle.

What will it look like if you execute your script better than ever? What will it feel like if you execute your script in the style of your dream game? What will others see?

Be clear about this – only from a place of relaxation can your intensity grow effectively. If you're too emotional, and if you over-think your game on the morning of a competitive match, your intensity will be shot to pieces come kick off. Your adrenaline resources will be drained, your energy sapped.

Picturing and mentally rehearsing your script is most effective when you do so approximately two hours before your match begins. In this way, a momentum of intensity can grow slowly, gently and effectively. Holding your script in your hands and chiselling it into your brain's pathways is your first mental step on match day.

Your Physical Warm Up

Your bars are full and your football brain is moulded in the shape of your script. You know what you have to do.

Now is the time to get your controllers out – your body and your self-talk. Now is the time to switch them on and ready them for extreme speed.

Every soccer player warms up physically. It's a non-negotiable. Nowadays everyone knows that you would be risking a horrendous injury if you didn't stretch, do some speed and agility work, get the feel of the ball and start to prepare your muscles to run, move, and twist, turn, kick, and tackle.

I hope that one day, we all have the same commitment to warming up our mindset alongside our body. I, for one, make this a fixed assignment for my players – they must use their physical warm up as a mental warm up. They must warm up their focus, their confidence, their belief, their distraction control, their emotional management, and their attention.

To do this, they have to use their controllers as soon as they start to get physical. I'd like you to do this too.

I'd like you to use your body controller. Start to become aware of every part of your body. Get on your toes, stand tall, and use positive gestures.

"On my toes, work, work, work, move, tall, move, head up, head up, tall, look, look, move, work"

Be constant on your body controller – be non-stop. The champion looks relentless. The champion, if he stands still, does so in a ready position. The champion is wide eyed, looking around, taking in information.

"Energy, keep going, keep working, look – left, look - right, move, move, on my toes, show for it"

If you find yourself switching off, then use your body controller to switch back on again – with speed. It's there to keep you feeling sharp, remaining persistent, and being ruthless. By using it, you can keep your attention, act with confidence, retain energy and manage emotion.

Add your self-talk controller into the mix. Instruct yourself as you play – not with complex language but with words from your script. You have a template related to the responsibilities within your role so if you get the chance, when doing a keep ball or small sided game, mentally practice your script. This is your time for a full dress rehearsal – you may as well make the most of the opportunity.

Create the blueprint you want to recreate as you warm up. Use your controllers to rehearse your script. Use your controllers to fire your body and charge your mind. When you do so, you will hit the sweetspot that lies somewhere in-between relaxation and intensity, and that rests somewhere between effort and calm.

The Final Ten

Loosen the grip you have on your controllers and slacken your intensity load. It's time to take a few deep breaths and relax your body. The final ten minutes before kick-off has arrived.

For many players this is when instruction from a coach starts to fly around the room and float in and out of players' awareness. It's important to listen to what your coach has to say – you must take on board instruction. But this is also a time for calmness, for coolness, for a still mind, for a relaxed body.

I'd like you to take some of this time to once again draw on your internal energy… to picture your script. You've revved your engines during warm up, now I'd like you to fine-tune your mindset by seeing your script in your mind's eye.

"What will it look like if I execute my script with confidence, with energy, with focus and with belief today?"

This is also when you could include a statement of intent:

"Today I am going to execute my script. That is all I can do. I can't force my performance. All I can do is focus on the plays in my script to be the very best I can be. I am going to use my controllers to perform my script. I am going to use my controllers with speed. I will be relentless with my body controller and I will use my self-talk controller to stick to my script. This is all I expect from myself – this is all I can do."

Now you are ready to go play. You are relaxed but focused. You know exactly what you are trying to achieve. You are confident and energised. You have left no stone unturned in readiness for kick-off.

Now you are ready to go play…

Technique Number 13
Create a match day routine, and make it routine!

14

ANA and the ANTs

So now, you've been through your pre-match routine and you've coated your mind and body with confidence.

"I'm ready to play. I can't force a great performance but I know I can play well by sticking to my match script and keeping my bars full. I have my two controllers – my self-talk and my body – and I know if I use them quickly then I can have a strong game."

Your physical warm up has fired up your mental muscles.

"Confident Lion – Strong, on my toes, positive, positive, work, stay tall, tall, tall – come on, be Confident Lion, be Confident lion"

"Agh gave it away – that was sloppy – forget that, be confident lion, stay sharp, come on sharp, lively, keep moving, move, move, move, look ready, be ready"

The last ten minutes before kick-off has affirmed your script.

"My script is to be Confident Lion. My first play is to stay on my toes no matter what – what does this look like? What does this feel like? My second play is to check where my man is at all times – what does this look like? My third play is to be vocal and support others – what does this look like?

Now it's time to play – remember what your goal is.

"All I can do is use my two controllers to execute my match script and keep my bars as high as possible. That is all I can do."

Be ready to use your controllers at all times. If you make a mistake, use your controllers to get back to your script. If you go a goal down, use your controllers to stay with your script and keep your confidence bar high. If you go a goal up, use your controllers to stick to your script and maintain a full energy bar.

"On my toes, stay positive, focus, focus, focus, my ball... be vocal – Confident lion, stay confident"

"Great tackle, stick with the script – Confident Lion, come on stay upbeat, stay positive, shoulders, where's my man, watch him..."

"Confident Lion - keep going, keep working, keep moving... stay tall, come on stay switched on, where's my man... stay with him, work, work, work, work..."

Of course, you won't speak to yourself like this while competing. Much of what you do will be instinctive and automatic.

But it's important to keep both your controllers close to hand. You will need them at regular intervals during the game. Even if you're standing still you can check in with your body controller. That may be using it to act alert, by being on your toes, or at least being ready to move.

- *To stay alert – act alert*
- *To stay sharp – act sharp*
- *To stay focused – act focused*
- *Use your body controllers – be it to become it*

Despite not having a running commentary in your head you have to use your self-talk controller at times to remind yourself of your script, as well as to maintain your energy bar and your confidence bar.

You have to be proactive with your self-talk because so many players are reactive. If I was to secretly insert a tape recorder in your head (one that had the facility to record your inner voice) I would want to hear sentences related to your script. I would want to hear words associated to the plays in your script – words that help drive you on, that slow you down when necessary, that increase intensity when you have to, that help you anticipate, move, adopt the right position and close down the opposition.

I'm passionate about the sentences and words you use as you play. They help you pay attention. They help you stay alert, alive and lively. They can boost your confidence, they can diminish irrelevant thoughts, and they can unchain you from the burden of distraction.

Champions in sport speak to themselves confidently. They act confidently. When others around them panic, they use their self-talk to send a pulse of calmness through their body. They act like a winner even when they are not winning. They display the attitude of a winner and they hold themselves like a winner irrespective of the score. That is why they are champions.

Champions use their self-talk and their body actions as they perform – they strive in every game to stay focused, confident, relaxed and competing at the right intensity by using a combination of their self-talk and body actions. They say it, they do it and they be it to become it!

This is why your self-talk and body controllers must become part of your footballing DNA. They are your chief self-regulators out on the pitch. You need them because competing in soccer isn't as straightforward as we'd like it to be. There are, in actual fact, two opponents on the pitch.

The first is the obvious – the opposing team you are playing against. The second is less apparent. It's those destructive thought patterns that can invade your mind as you play. These inner demons surface because of the way the brain works – not just in football but in life too. Let's take a closer look at how they can impact upon your performance by taking a microscopic look at the most important muscle you possess.

A Brain Called ANA

Your brain is never quiet. It's a cacophony of noise. If you had a chance to take a look at the electrical activity of your brain, it would be like looking down from outer space at electrical storms striking the surface of the earth. The brain is constantly alight, alive and lively. And the result is a never ending flow of thoughts and images vying for attention in your conscious mind.

This is a process brain scientists call Ambient Neural Activity, or ANA for short. I'm often asked by clients why it is so difficult to turn off the inner narrative that can so often distract on the pitch. It's because the connections in your brain are constantly connecting, processing and re-connecting. They do so without break or interruption as you go about your everyday life.

This is one of the reasons why concentration in sport is such a challenge. You can be playing soccer and all kinds of thoughts can invade your mind. Perhaps you've noticed this.

I once worked with a client who competed in the EPL. Playing in front of 40,000 people a week his brain would pop a song into his mind and it would get stuck. He would be singing to himself as he competed.

Do your thoughts flit and fly and float as you compete? Do you tend to have thoughts pop into your mind that distract you?

Not only can random thoughts invade you, but ANA also works to throw thoughts into your conscious mind after something has happened on the pitch – after you've scored, gone a goal down, made a mistake, completed a pass, given the ball away and other such actions that happen over the course of 90 minutes. Because of ANA, we are constantly judging what is going on around us as we play and compete.

- *"I can't believe I missed that opportunity, I'm never going to score today"*
- *"A goal up already, we're flying"*
- *"Agh, terrible pass. I hope I'm not going to have one of those days"*
- *"Great ball – that feels awesome"*

The brain marches a quick beat as you play. In fact, it creates thoughts in milliseconds – instantaneous reactions and responses to events as they unfold on the pitch. ANA is quick and can be deadly to your game. You have to deal with it. You have to manage the brain's impulse to throw unwanted thoughts into your game and to make judgments after every play. Why? Because ANA gives birth to the ANTs.

ANTs

In Soccer Tough, I introduced you to the concept of ANTs.

ANTs is an acronym for Automatic Negative Thoughts. These thoughts eat away at your focus and sap your confidence. When they linger, they tighten your body and feed you doubt and worry and fear. They are a common feature of the competitive mindset because, under pressure, the brain loves to work against you. It doesn't like to work rationally, it's just not designed to. It's there to warn you about the danger – the fact you've made a mistake or gone a goal down. The fact the referee is making decisions against you or the fact the opposition is looking mighty strong.

The brain loves to bookmark failure. It has evolved to direct your attention towards the problems you encounter on the pitch. And when our focus is captured by these problems, so the ANTs pile up.

"I can't believe I made that mistake… I'm playing awful… if I keep this up I'm going to be dropped… and if I'm dropped I'll never get back in the team"

One ANT can multiply quickly. A single, small negative statement can reproduce into dozens of self-critical thoughts that prevent you from playing with focus and freedom and stop you from competing with coordination, timing, and fluidity.

Combined, those thoughts can cause us to play with fear and trepidation. They can cause us to play with too much care or with an indecisive mind. Great soccer players must have a squashing process to deal with the ANTs that invade their mind and their game.

The Squashing Process

In Soccer Tough, I gave you a simple way to squash ANTs, and here I'm going to reinforce my SPOT STOP SHIFT principle of dealing with your inner bugs. It's simple, it's quick, and it's effective.

SPOT – STOP – SHIFT

In Soccer Tough, I introduced the reader to the classic psychological technique of thought stopping. It's simple but powerful. It works! For those of you who are unfamiliar with this technique, let's take a look at this method of squashing ANTs.

To be able to squash the ANT you need to SPOT it first. You need to be aware of it and I ask all the players I work with to spend time on the training ground identifying when and where they have ANTs.

Some have them when they make mistakes. Others tend to experience them when they are losing or even when others make errors. I have worked with players whose ANTs tend to revolve around their future in the game. When they're competing they get worried about being substituted or being left out of the team in the next game.

I have helped players to deal with ANTs related to the opposition. Defenders can face ANTs that relate to the qualities of opposition strikers – they are too quick, too strong and too good. Strikers, on the other hand, may weave a story in their mind about how powerful and lively the defenders are.

Whatever the contents of your ANTs, for you to be able to deal with them you must develop the skill of SPOTTING the ANT. This is no easy task. Most of your football will be played on autopilot. Just as you may be unaware of the physical habits you portray on the pitch, you may be equally oblivious to the mental patterns that underpin every decision, every action and every motion you take. A footballer needs to develop the capacity to recognize how he is talking to himself. He needs to notice when he is thinking in a manner that is destructive to his game. Or as I like to say: "SPOT the ANT"

STOP

The next stage is to STOP the ANT. SPOT then STOP! In other words your task is to STOP your negative inner voice from taking shape and affecting your runs, movement, vision, awareness and focus.

In my experience, the quicker a soccer player stops negative thoughts the more effective this technique is. When a footballer allows an ANT to linger the more destructive it becomes. One ANT is quickly joined by other ANTs.

- *"I'm playing awful today... I never play well against this team... I'm going to be dropped."*
- *"This striker is way too quick... I'm going to concede soon... I'm going to let my team mates down."*

STOPPING ANTs is simple, in theory, but difficult in practice. What I like to get players to do is to envisage a STOP sign in their mind. Imagine a big red STOP sign, like the ones you see on the side of the road.

An alternative is to say STOP to yourself. You can scream it in your mind if you want. STOP! What you need is something that you can consciously see, or say, that will snap you back into the present moment and instantly stop the ANTs from spreading.

Just as SPOTTING requires practice and patience so does STOPPING. Once you feel comfortable spotting ANTs – start to stop them. Do this in training. The more you practice, the better you'll become at taking control of your ANTs.

SHIFT

So, you've SPOTTED the ANT and you've STOPPED the ANT – now you have to SHIFT the ANT. You have to SHIFT your negative thoughts to something more helpful and something more constructive.

To make sense of the idea of SHIFTING, I'd like you to try this mini experiment right now. For the next ten seconds, I'd like you to think about your bedroom at home. What does this look like? Get an image of it in your mind. Now I'd like you to shift to thinking about the kitchen in your home. What does it look like? Get an inner image of your kitchen.

This may be really obvious but let's think about what you've just done. Your mind has the capacity to shift between thoughts. I can, intentionally, move my focus of attention from one thing to another, more often than not in a seamless manner.

Now I'd like you to do the same with an image of your best soccer and your worst soccer. For a few seconds, think about yourself at your best, and then for the next few seconds think about you at your worst. You see, again, you get to direct what you place your attention on.

Now play about with your focus of attention and the direction of your thinking. For ten seconds, focus on your family members then for the next ten seconds think about your closest friends. Take ten seconds to think about your favourite place and then ten seconds to focus on your favourite film.

I ask you to do these tasks because I want you to understand that everyone has the ability to SHIFT their thoughts, and I want you to recognise what shifting feels like.

For you to become the very best soccer player you can be, you must have the capacity to shift in the moment. After you've SPOTTED the ANT and STOPPED the ANT, you must SHIFT the ANT with extreme speed. With lightning speed.

This is because you don't want the ANT to nest and give birth to more ANTs. You don't want an infestation of ANTs that damages your technique, slows you down, lessens your movement, reduces your runs, and eats away at your confidence.

Like my clients, I want you to know that you *can* SHIFT away from distraction and shift away from an overly negative mindset. You *can* SHIFT away from a focus on past mistakes. You *can* SHIFT away from irrelevant thoughts.

There are several ways to do this and I've always found that different players employ differing methods to SHIFT their ANTs. No one size fits all! Here are the four shifts you can make:

1. SHIFT to Match Script
2. SHIFT to Positive body actions
3. SHIFT to Confident self-talk
4. SHIFT to Helpful self-talk

The first and most obvious way is to SHIFT back to your match script. By using your self-talk to return to your script you are engaging in a game relevant focus. This is a particularly simple and powerful way to deal with ANTs that are related to irrelevant thoughts, and thoughts about mistakes.

- *"That was a terrible mistake, STOP, let's get back to my script"*
- *"Such an unfair decision by the referee, STOP, let's stick to my script"*
- *"I can't believe coach is having a go at me for that, STOP, just stick to my script"*

In this way, there is no internal discussion about the situation. There is no inner debate about the fairness or unfairness of anything that's just happened. You simply direct your brain attention to what is most important to you – your script.

Similarly, a SHIFT to positive body actions avoids any argument with yourself. It's a neat, quick and brutal process. As soon as you hear the ANT, you STOP and SHIFT by doing something with your body. The choice is up to you and there's no right or wrong bodily solution.

- *"I can't believe we're a goal down, STOP, (SHIFT onto my toes)"*
- *"I'm just playing so poorly today, STOP, (SHIFT by being vocal)"*
- *"There's no way we can win this today, STOP (SHIFT stay tall and act sharp)"*

Just the very process of placing your attention on your body and doing something with your torso is enough to squash the ANT before an infestation takes hold of mind and body.

A lot of my clients love keeping it this simple. They enjoy the fact that they know they can stay in control of themselves and keep their performance free-flowing by squashing the inevitable ANTs that they have, by getting back to their match script or by doing something positive with their body. This gives them a sense of ease as they go into battle.

"I know I'll have ANTs out there and, when I do, I know exactly how to squash them. It's okay to have ANTs, I just have to make sure I deal with them. I have to make sure I SPOT them quickly, STOP them with speed and SHIFT them by using my self-talk to get back to my match script or by using my body controller to focus on doing something positive with my body actions. That's so simple – I know I can do that. I know I am in complete control."

Confident Shifting

Your self-talk controller is a really robust piece of equipment. You can use it to help you SHIFT back to the match script and you can use it to remind your body controller to help you dance your feet.

I also like my players to be flexible enough to use their self-talk in other ways. I like them to engage in confident SHIFTING from time to time.

Talking to yourself confidently on the pitch – that 'can do' attitude – is a decisive factor in drowning the negativity that pervades when the ANTs set in. For many of my players, simply speaking to themselves positively is essential if they are to remain in control and compete with confidence.

I'd like you to build your portfolio of ANT squashing by adding the ability to speak to yourself confidently.

- *"I can't keep up with this striker, STOP, I CAN"*

- *"I'm never going to score today, STOP, I WILL"*
- *"I'm just not good enough for this team, STOP, I AM"*

Speak to yourself confidently, with energy. Shout to your inner self if you have to. I'd like you to imagine that you have a tape recorder in your head. If we played this tape back after a match we'd hear 'can do' words. We'd hear strong and powerful words. We'd hear words that keep you going, keep you moving, and keep you relentless no matter what.

I can, I will, and I am, are just as important as ball control, passing, shooting and tackling. They are just as important as awareness and anticipation. This is because these actions are built on a bed of confidence and motivation. Without the soft skills, it's tough to develop the hard skills. When you learn to speak to yourself effectively, you give yourself a better chance to trap and control the ball like a professional. The fundamental skills in football are put at risk without the basics of inner language.

Your job on the pitch isn't just to survive, it's to thrive. It's to play with freedom. It's to express. It's to lead. It's to compete with passion and poise. You sculpt these indispensable attitudes into your soccer CV and you need to be an "I can" player. You need to be an "I will" and an "I am" player.

Helpful Shifting

Of course, positive self-talk is important, but soccer players need to be intelligent about their football as well. They need to find solutions to the problems that arise as the game plays out.

Football is a game of momentum that swings back and forth in tune with the subtle personal victories that happen all over the pitch. A big part of your job is to help your team steal momentum and keep it, as well as deal effectively with moments when momentum is against you.

The ANTs you experience that relate to being outplayed by an opposite number must be met with a set of helpful strategies. If your team mates aren't doing what they're supposed to do, then it's your job to squash any ANTs you have related to the problem; find a solution and play.

- *"This player is so quick, STOP, I'm just going to have to leave a little more space between myself and her, and not commit so quickly. I know this means she might get a cross in, but I've just got to focus on the perfect time to commit myself."*
- *"Wow, it's going to be tough to keep a clean sheet today, STOP, this means I have to make sure I'm really vocal and command my area more. I've got to stay on my toes and make sure my defenders see me lead as a goalkeeper."*
- *"The wingers aren't making quick breaks like they're supposed to, STOP, I've just got to keep my passes simple. It also means I've got to work harder in the middle of the park. The wingers were asked to make those breaks but maybe they're lacking confidence. I just need to work hard off the ball and try and retain possession as much as I can."*

A great player finds solutions in the blink of an eye and carries on. To give yourself a chance to play smart soccer you can't allow yourself to build an ANT farm in your mind. As soon as you SPOT the problem you have to SHIFT it by considering solutions and being ready to apply the answer.

The Quick and the Dead

Speed on the football pitch isn't reserved for the physical side of the game. Speed in soccer is also a mental requirement. A sharp mind – a mind ready to switch on, in an instant – is a pre-requisite for superior performance. Footballers not only need an athletic body, but also a nimble, athletic mind.

The speed of the soccer brain needs to be raw. It needs to be like a jab and duck from Floyd Mayweather. It needs to be similar to Lewis Hamilton shifting into sixth gear. Ideally, it's as quick as Usain Bolt once he's into his stride.

I want to set you a challenge. I want you to become world class at squashing ANTs. This means SPOTTING them, stopping them, and then shifting them quicker and quicker and quicker. It means going through this squashing process in the time it takes me to snap my finger or clap my hand.

Never, ever, let an ANT settle. That's Soccer Timid, and I want nothing less than Soccer Tough. The quicker you can squash your ANTs, the less they can impede your game. And the more you practice your squashing techniques, the more accustomed you will become in picking the right shift in the moment.

In soccer, you are either quick on the distraction draw, or you are dead. This may sound over the top but this is how I like my clients to see it. I like them to see ANTs as the kind of pest that can play havoc with their game, so much so that they put the skill of squashing them on a pedestal. Taking a no compromise attitude may not stamp out ANTs for good, but you will certainly prevent the kind of infestation that leads to slumps.

Just as a boxer shifts his feet at lightning pace to dodge a punch, so I want you dodging distraction by building the skill of squashing ANTs with speed. The footballer with a quiet mind, free from ANTs, sets his feet and legs and torso free. He can have fun. He can play to win and not to lose. He can play on the front foot and not the back foot. He can play with freedom and not with fear. He can be aggressive when he wants and defensive when he wants. That's a great footballing skill to have.

Technique Number 14

Squash ANTs with Speed.

15

BLR Ronaldo

His script is prepared. Controllers are set. Yannick Bolasie is on his feet and ready to play. But before he takes to the pitch he allows his inner voice to direct his attention:

"BLR Ronaldo...

Come on BLR Ronaldo...

BLR – brave, lively, relentless...

Brave – what does this look like? Feel like? Take the full back on, drive at him and make him scared - brave, brave, brave...

Lively – stay switched on at all times. Get this going in warm up, on my toes, alert, alive and lively. Remember my body controller. Into the action – be sharp. Always 'What next'.

Relentless – never give in. Make a mistake, stay relentless. Give the ball away, stay relentless. Relentless with my runs, relentless with my crosses, a relentless mindset to kill the confidence of the defenders.

Ronaldo – yes Ronaldo – what does it look like if I'm Ronaldo? What does it feel like? What would others see?"

His self-talk is determined and aligned with the script he's set himself, while his body controller is kicking in – he's on his toes, his head is up and his eyes are steely focused.

Of course, despite this intensity, he knows he cannot force his performance. He knows a great match is born through a keen balance of relaxation and effort. To impose himself on the opposition he has to be clear-minded and physically loose.

This is why Yannick goes through his script in minute detail before he walks out in front of a stadium packed full of fans. To empty his mind he allows his thoughts to settle on how he wants to play, who he wants to be, and how he wants to direct his game.

On this day, 11th April 2015, the Crystal Palace winger is preparing himself to play at the Stadium of Light. It is Palace versus Sunderland, an especially important match for Sunderland who are finding themselves sucked into a relegation scrap at the end of a long, arduous season. They will fight and the Palace players are aware of this.

In the away changing room, Yannick is continuing to talk to himself.

"I haven't scored enough goals and I know I need to score more. But all I can do is be BLR Ronaldo. All I can do is use my two controllers – my self-talk and body actions. I've worked hard in training. I trust that BLR Ronaldo will help me to score."

BLR Ronaldo is the statement Yannick has chosen to condense all the plays in his script. These single words (brave, lively and relentless) and this solitary name (Ronaldo) mask a whole bunch of runs, movements and responsibilities that he must strive to get right. When he whispers them to himself, he sees his role come alive. These words become pictures in his mind. The pictures create a blueprint of how he wants to play and inject confidence through his body.

"BLR Ronaldo – what does this look like? What does this feel like? I can be BLR Ronaldo. I will be BLR Ronaldo no matter what. BLR Ronaldo is what I am. It is what I do."

Yala

When I was called in to help Yannick 'Yala' Bolasie establish himself as a Premier League player, I was unaware of his precocious ability. I was unaware of the dancing feet that left defenders in a whirl. I was unaware of his pace, power and perseverance. These are qualities I soon became acquainted with.

We had a strong start to our footballing relationship. In our first season of work, Yannick took to my methodologies quickly. He had some great performances against top teams. One in particular made the back page headlines.

In a display of incredible energy, he broke the hearts of Liverpool players and fans as an amazing 15 minutes of soccer saw Crystal Palace come back from three-nil down to draw three all. Yannick, who had been quiet up until the 75 minute mark played a spectacular final 15.

Playing brave and lively and relentless helped him surge deep into the Liverpool half time and time again. His tireless work rate and penetrating crosses set up goals for his team mates. The mantra of BLR Ronaldo had impacted the game and consequently the outcome of the season beyond what we thought possible (the dropped points meant Liverpool went on to lose the Premier League and Manchester City were crowned champions a week later.)

So Yannick continued to perform consistently. He continued to impress and build a reputation for being a fast, tricky and dangerous Premier League winger. And our relationship continued into a second season where he diligently worked at his training script, improved his ability to use his controllers with speed, and maintained his match script mantra of BLR Ronaldo. And then in mid-April 2015 he arrived with the team in Sunderland.

Eleven Heaven

Whenever a Premier League footballer stands in the tunnel waiting to walk out onto the pitch he doesn't know what's going to happen. He'd like to play well but he can't guarantee it. And when Yannick stood in the tunnel at the Stadium of Light, the home ground of Sunderland, he wasn't to know about the spectacular game that was about to unfold. He had, however, a happy place to visit. As he strode out onto the pitch he immersed himself in BLR Ronaldo. He *became* BLR Ronaldo.

The first half was quiet in terms of goals – a nil-nil stalemate at the break prompted Crystal Palace to start the second half with energy and pace. And this is when BLR Ronaldo really came into his own.

In the 47th minute, BLR Ronaldo, in a free role working both wings sent a teasing cross in for Palace striker Glenn Murray to nod home the opener. Then it was BLR Ronaldo's turn to go on a scoring blitz.

A ball from deep and a flick-on from Murray in minute 50 saw BLR Ronaldo in the box with space. The space had opened up through BLR Ronaldo's *lively* movement and *relentless* search for gaps in the defence. Pulling away from the defender, BLR Ronaldo slotted the ball home with ease.

Then, just two minutes later, BLR Ronaldo made a *brave* run at a ball played over the top of Sunderland defender John O'Shea. *Relentlessly* strong and powerful BLR Ronaldo shrugged off the Irish defender and lobbed the keeper in true *Ronaldo* style.

Finally, in minute 61, great work from Murray helped the striker deliver a pass to BLR Ronaldo in the middle of the penalty area. The goalkeeper came out quickly to smother any shot but BLR Ronaldo remained *brave* and *lively* and *relentless*, and despite two defenders encroaching on his space, his stretched foot sent the ball into the back of the next.

An incredible 11 minute hat-trick for BLR Ronaldo – Brave Lively Relentless Ronaldo – executed by Yannick Bolasie.

When you play, I want you to play in the style of your script. I want you to use your two controllers to act out your script. I want you to use your self-talk and body actions to keep your confidence bar full and maintain your energy bar as best you can.

What does this look like? What does this feel like? What will others see?

Fun, Freedom and Focus

The next time you tune into a match that Yannick plays I want you to watch him and reflect on the thinking that underpins his game.

Yannick isn't going to have a great game every time and it might be that you watch one of his quieter performances. But guess what – he's still striving to be the very best he can be. He's still doing the things he has to do to have a great game. Of course, it doesn't always work out that a great process leads to a great performance. It's not always two plus two makes four. It just doesn't operate like that and Yannick is aware of this. He knows he can only massage the main event by being the best he can be with his script and his controllers.

- *He can't make a team mate pass to him. He can only show for it and vocalise his desire for the ball.*
- *He can't force a goal. He can only do the things that are going to help him score – specifically being brave and lively and relentless with his movement and runs.*
- *He can't make himself man of the match – he can't control that. He can only stick to his script to give him the best chance of executing his responsibilities with power and energy and effort.*

This is the same for your soccer. You can't force it. Provided you have your script in place, your bars full and your controllers fit for purpose, you can't do anymore.

When you watch Yannick play, you will be watching a footballer immersed in his script. You will be watching a player striving to use his controllers. You will be watching a soccer player who has prepared for the game by building his confidence and energy bars and charging his inner batteries. Does that mean he'll be incredible? It doesn't guarantee it. He can only but try to be the very best he can be, on any particular day, and in any particular match.

I reinforce this idea because so many soccer players try far too hard. They try to force their performance. They misunderstand the notion of a 'winning mentality' and the idea of 'being up for it'. As a consequence, their overexertion leads to tension, tightness and tiredness. They compete with little sense of freedom and their focus is dispersed and often distracted. This can not only lead to a poor performance but can also restrain enjoyment.

Those types of players might be interested to know that underpinning the BLR Ronaldo match script are another three words that Yannick and I often discuss. They are three words that I talk about, at length, about in Soccer Tough, and they are three words that I use with most of my clients.

Underpinning Yannick's ability to execute BLR Ronaldo are fun, freedom and focus.

Yannick always tries to play with a smile on his face. He still wants to win, but he understands that to give himself a chance to win he has to enjoy himself. To give himself a chance to play well he has to feel good.

Playing with a smile on the face isn't for everyone, but I ask all my clients to go out and have fun. I ask them to experience excitement and entertainment as they compete. I want them to feel excited about going a goal up. I want them to feel excitement about having to come back from a goal down. I want them to summon up excitement if they make a couple of mistakes – "Today is going to be a challenge. It's going to be a challenge to compete at my best because right now things aren't happening. But that's okay. Let's have fun striving to get back into the game."

Think about why you started playing soccer with your mates in the first place? It was fun. It was exciting. It was pleasurable. It was enjoyable. It was entertaining. Keep it that way. Keep it that way no matter what.

It is the attitude of fun that leads to greatness. Fun takes risks. Fun explores. Fun experiments. Fun delivers on competitiveness. When I watch Ronaldo and Messi play, I see the look of fun follow their face and the feeling of fun exerted through their body. Sure, they may look serious on the pitch but they're still having a whole lot of fun.

"I play with fun – what does this look like? What does this feel like? What will others see?"

Combined with having fun, I want Yannick to play with freedom. I want him to play loose and free. I want him to shake away the nerves and the tension and allow ripples of freedom to break through his legs and through his torso. It's the same torso that is going to spend 90 minutes swaying and swerving around the bodies of the opposition. It's the same torso that's going to commit and create. It needs to be free from stress and rigidity and anxiety.

"I play with complete freedom – what does this look like? What does this feel like? What will others see?"

Yannick gets it. He knows he needs an undercoat of freedom if he is going to play BLR Ronaldo. He also knows that whilst there are risks if he plays with unabashed freedom, there is a greater risk if he plays with fear. The crippling effects of doubt and worry will prevent him from positively impacting the game.

Interestingly, there are lots of coaches I've spoken with who wince at the idea of their players competing with freedom. They relate freedom to being careless, to the point of being reckless.

When I talk about playing with freedom, I speak with an eye on a footballer's role. I speak with a head nod towards a player's responsibilities. A footballer can play with freedom and yet still be disciplined. Freedom isn't sloppy or headless or chaotic or careless or rash. You can play with freedom within the confines of your position. You can play with a sense of freedom yet still be committed to a specific set of instructions that you must not veer from.

The opposite of freedom is fear. I don't want my clients playing with fear. I know that if Yannick lined up overly fearful of the opposition – say against the likes of a Manchester City or an Arsenal – then his movement would be stifled and his runs would be limited. On the contrary, Yannick wants to express himself on the pitch. He strives to play with freedom no matter what. This can take the form of a weaving run or a constant stream of movement. But, equally, his brand of freedom can be woven into a simple pass or easy header. Freedom comes in many forms!

To emphasise the importance of instruction and discipline I would add focus to freedom. The focus comes shaped as a match script. I want players focused on the script as they compete. The moves, plays and actions they make should, within reason, be confined to their script.

"I focus on my script. I stay glued to my script at all times. I am relentless with my script. I execute my script with fun, freedom and focus. What does this look like? What does this feel like? What would others see if I do this?"

A footballer with a focused mind also pays attention to her confidence and energy bars, as well as utilising her controllers to maintain the script. She comes back to it at times of distraction.

It really is that simple. Crank up the volume of fun and enjoy yourself. Be expressive and play with freedom, and focus your mind on your script, your bars and your controllers. The combination of fun, freedom and focus provide the perfect blend of effort and relaxation. Combined, they provide the base for an energetic and passionate display, as well as an intelligent and thoughtful performance.

This is how Yannick Bolasie likes to play his football. This is how he delivers on match day time and time again. He consciously immerses himself in his script and melds himself into a feeling of fun, freedom and focus. This helps him find the perfect blend of thinking and doing. Let's now talk more about that perfect mix.

Technique Number 15

Execute your match script with fun, freedom and focus.

16

Playing 80/20

I ask my clients to play in the present moment as best they can. To my mind, the present moment (within the context of soccer) means the now and the next five seconds.

A mind truly fixed in the present doesn't dwell on what's been. It doesn't reflect on the goal that's just gone in or the pass that was made a few moves earlier. It doesn't orientate itself to the controversial refereeing decision from 5 minutes earlier. And it moves on from the heavy tackle made that led to a yellow card not long before.

Similarly, attention in the present has no room for the future beyond the next five seconds. The tough second half isn't relevant when you're immersed in the first throws of the game. What the coach will say to you at half-time is something the present mind cannot abide. Playing now and reading the next five seconds is the preoccupation of the champion soccer player.

This is harder to do than many appreciate. The brain loves to direct itself forwards and backwards. It enjoys dwelling on the worst of what's just been. It likes to project ahead to the problems the game holds.

I ask my clients to practice playing soccer in the present moment every time they take to a pitch. Holding onto a match script, a training script, using controllers, and squashing ANTs all help to make this tough-to-reach state possible. Becoming accomplished at self-regulation and self-control is an everyday challenge that you have to try and win.

The battle to find this state of mind is something that Henry Molaison never struggled with. In fact, he slipped into it all day, every day.

You have probably never heard of Henry. I don't think he ever kicked a soccer ball and I'm not sure he was even a fan of the beautiful game. But in spite of this, his intriguing (and sad) story provides us with a lesson of how footballers should enjoy playing the game. Here is the story of Henry Molaison.

The Molaison Memory

In 1953, at the age of 27, Henry Molaison lost his memory and forever stayed in the present moment. It happened after a surgical procedure to try to cure epileptic seizures that he'd been suffering since he was 16-years-old.

The operation attempted to remove the parts of the brain that doctors thought were causing his fits. Unfortunately, the procedure went wrong and Henry lost what psychologists call his declarative memory.

Whilst Henry retained a little about life before having surgery, every experience gained *after* the operation – facts presented to him and things that happened to him- were forgotten within 30 seconds. He could remember some things about his childhood, but if you had asked him to pick up a book and 30 seconds later recall what he had just read, he would be unable to do it.

Worst of all, his caregivers had to introduce themselves to him every day as he had no idea who they were. The doctors and nurses that looked after him were forever strangers to Henry.

Amazingly, his friendly personality and intelligent demeanour remained intact, and he allowed psychologists to examine him to learn more about the human brain and memory. And there was something, in particular, they found interesting.

It had become apparent that whilst Henry had lost his ability to remember consciously, not all of his daily memory faculties had been destroyed. It appeared that he was able to learn new skills without really knowing it.

This was demonstrated through specially designed psychology tests, one of which was a motor skill test. Specifically, Henry had to draw lines between points in star-like patterns. He was asked to do this several times over the course of a day and as he did so, he would make fewer errors the more he practiced it.

In short, he was learning a new motor skill despite not being consciously aware of doing anything different or anything better.

What these tests demonstrated was that different memories are housed in different areas of the brain. Conscious memories require the area that was destroyed in Henry's brain. But memories of learned motor skills reside in a different area of the brain – in the deeper levels of the unconscious mind.

Two Brains, Two States of Play

Champion athletes perform the majority of the time using this unconscious mind. It's the area that holds all the memories of their skills that they build from training and playing and practicing. This area enables them to just do! No thinking, just doing!

Take a few minutes to hold a video image of how the best footballers on the planet play. They play loose and free and uninhibited. They enjoy unrestricted motion and boundless movement.

When you watch a Messi or Wambach or Ronaldo play well, they are – by and large – playing unconsciously. They immerse themselves in a bubble of unconscious play. They are trusting the repetition gained from thousands of hours of training. There is very little thinking, there is a lot of doing. There is very little judgment, there is a lot of action.

The mazy runs that skilful players make aren't met with a barrage of noise from the brain. They are not talking their way through the opposition, they are simply going through them. They are not saying, "Go left, side-foot right, stop, start, flick." They are just doing these things on auto-pilot, relying on unconscious memory as they have been practiced so many times before.

When you play soccer, I'd like you to compete most of the time in an unconscious mode. I'd like you to allow the deeper parts of your brain to guide you. You've trained hard and I want you to trust that training. Have fun and be free. Enjoy the sensation of 'just doing'.

"But hold on," I hear you cry. "You've given me a self-talk controller. I now have a script. In the last chapter, you told me that Yannick Bolasie and all your other clients 'talk' to themselves before they play and as they compete. You've told me to think about my body language and my bodily actions. You've asked me to use my controllers to keep my energy bars high. Now you're telling me not to think? Now you're telling me to just do? Please explain."

The Unconscious/Conscious Sweet-spot

I ask players to play unconsciously 80% of the time. I want them to play consciously 20% of the time. I want them to strike a keen balance between their unconscious and conscious. I'm going to use examples from another sport to highlight what I mean.

In tennis, Roger Federer or Serena Williams play 80/20. 80% of the time they trust their training and let their shots take care of themselves. They don't think about how far they're going to take the racket back and they don't consciously focus on the angle the racket head hits the ball. They let the motion take care of itself. If they were to overly think about these things during play they'd never get the ball over the net!

However, there are things that champion tennis players *do* consciously think about. They will have a set of tactics to beat an opponent. They will be constantly aware of these tactics. Tennis players will also choose where they're going to serve the ball – they consciously consider a type of serve to hit. And players will also use their controllers. You may have seen them at Wimbledon or at Flushing Meadows talking to themselves as they start to lose or encourage themselves as they win a few games in a row. They will know that a slump in body language is going to cause them to get too down on themselves. They will consciously keep themselves upbeat, ready and sharp.

Tennis players compete 80/20. If this balance is lost, it prevents them playing at their best. Too much instinct (90/10) and they'll lose their ability to think appropriately in the moment. They'll make sloppy decisions and they'll fail to recognise when they need to gee themselves up, calm themselves down, or shift their focus in a different direction. In contrast, too much thought and an over-control of shots will prevent them from playing a free flowing, winning game. Their shots will be erratic and their mind fogged and preoccupied.

This is no different in football. I don't think there's any argument that a game of soccer needs to be played without too much thought. It requires an instinctive mind. But a footballer needs to use her conscious mind as well. She needs to set out a game plan that includes the tactical, technical and mental components of the game, and she needs to condense them into simple-to-remember prompts that will focus her mind come kick off. This is the match script. She needs to observe when she has an ANT and intentionally squash it. She needs to recognise when she's switched off and re-focus her mind quickly. She needs to keep herself confident and energised as she competes.

Soccer players who compete 100% unconsciously can make mistakes without ever realising it. They can be sloppy. They can lose personal battles time and time again without striving to do anything to change the situation.

100% unconscious is directionless and too out of control. A soccer player needs an inner map of the behaviours he wants and the self-regulation techniques he can employ should he experience ANTs.

Xavi

When Xavi was growing up at La Masia, the Barcelona Academy, he was always thinking. Whenever he took to the pitch, he was thinking. The coaches set up training exercises to force him to think, but it was his own personal demands that drove him to "Think, think, think".

He would think about space – finding space. He would think about the movement of the opposition. He would think about the movement of his team mates. He would think about body shape, positioning, and the most effective runs to make.

He would train 50/50 – 50% unconsciously, 50% consciously. Of course, when he plays now this has calmed to 80/20, but for him to play to the very best of his ability he will still demand some thinking from himself. He will still look around and play 20% consciously.

The mazy runs he makes and the instinctive passes he executes will have been embedded into the depths of his brain after so many years of practice and performing, so for 80% of the match he is looking and doing. But for him to be a match winner he still needs to stick to a script with plays related to finding space, he still needs to keep himself focused and playing with freedom. He still needs to squash any ANTs that may arise as the game progresses.

Consciously Unconscious

Maybe the best way to describe how I want you to play is *consciously unconscious*. I want you to utilise your *conscious* mind to get the very most from your *unconscious* performance.

Play to compete with fun and freedom. Express and enjoy yourself. Be loose and confident and uninhibited. Look and do, look and do, look and do.

But to be able to stay in an unconscious mental state of 'look and do', and to get the very most out of this state, it's important to use your controllers to stay alert, alive and focused. It's important to remind yourself of your script from time to time. It's important to consciously squash any ANTs that your brain pushes through to your awareness.

The match kicks off. You unconsciously start to move and look around you. Even in the first minute, you can consciously use your self-talk controller to remind yourself of your script. Now you look and do – no thought – just look and do. Then, as you see the ball break up the pitch you unconsciously make your run – you look and do. The winger crosses it in and you automatically leap for the ball and get your head on it, but it goes wide. You hold your head in your hands for a couple of seconds, then you consciously remind yourself that you have to get back into your position quickly. You tell yourself you'll get another chance soon – great self-talk to keep yourself confident and focused.

The champion soccer player uses his self-talk and body controllers to keep himself going, keep himself focused, keep himself confident, and keep himself at the right intensity whilst competing unconsciously. He gets that magical 80/20 combo of excellence as he plays. He uses his conscious mind to get the very most out of his natural unconscious game.

Check-Ins

One effective way to play consciously unconscious is to consistently monitor your mindset as you compete. I ask my players to have regular check-ins as they perform. When the ball is out of play, I want them to ask themselves, "Am I sticking to my script? Am I using my controllers? Am I keeping my energy bars full?" I want them to become accustomed to monitoring their script, controllers, and bars to get the very most from their unconscious performance.

These check-ins can be decisive and quick. There isn't much time in a game of soccer to dwell on how well you're doing or how the game is unfolding. It's not a sport like golf where the pace of play allows for deliberation and unhurried reflection.

Start becoming skilled at the speedy check-in. The more you do it, the quicker you'll get at it. When the ball is up the other end of the pitch, when it's out of play, or when there is a short break in play, turn up the volume of your thoughts related to your script, your controllers, and bars. Go conscious on your unconscious.

Of course, the easiest and most obvious time to check-in is during half time. This is when you can give your game a thorough examination. Rather than giving way to the emotion of the score or the quality of yours and your team's performance, create an inner assessment of how well you're sticking to your script. Ask yourself where your bars are and how well you're using your controllers to be the very best you can be.

Half time is the period to go conscious. It's the time to analyse the good and the not so good. I strongly advise keeping this analysis related to your script, bars and controllers. Avoid getting overly complicated with your assessment – you'll only confuse yourself.

If your coach has some feedback, listen keenly. It's important to add your coach's thoughts to your script. If you have to make a change to your script then accept it – be flexible. The coach is in charge and he or she is providing you with a window into what better looks like.

Once it comes time to play the second half, be ready to go consciously unconscious again. Move your feet, get on your toes, lift your head up and prepare to play with fun and freedom. Turn up the volume of your focus and mentally have your script to hand so your conscious mind can steer you in the right direction for the next half.

Pressure Play

The footballer who is ready to play consciously unconscious – who is ready to perform 80/20 – is one who can get the very most from her performance. She can be flexible. When momentum is with her team, she can ride the wave of unconscious confidence. And when momentum shifts against her team – which inevitably will happen several times in every game – she can check-in with her conscious thoughts by using her controllers to deal with the pressure that is placed upon her and her team mates.

Champion footballers are pressure players. And pressure players have a keen mix of the instinctive and the deliberate. To be the very best you can be, you have to learn to play under the most intense pressure, whether that's a cup final, a promotion or relegation battle, a trial game or a match played in front of hundreds or thousands of fans. We'll now explore how you can learn to be a better soccer player under pressure.

Technique Number 16

Play 80/20 – use your conscious mind to get the
most out of your unconscious game.

17

Nervenstaerke

Their heart rates remain unaltered despite the life changing moment. A series of composed responses to a highly-charged few minutes that determines the trajectory of the players and the team.

The ice men, dressed in white, stand close to the centre circle watching team mate after team mate find the back of the net in one of the most high pressured sporting environments.

The sudden death penalty kick out suits the ice men – cold, calculating and intelligent – they know how to hold their nerve. They know about nervenstaerke.

Each player walks to the penalty spot with a laser-like focus, no doubts, with only the back of the net in mind. The ball is placed with authority, their heart rate is calm, a perfect picture of success formed in their mind. Then the run up.

The gritty stare, no doubts, only net. A goal!

The German National team have never lost a penalty shoot-out in the World Cup and have missed only one attempt from 18 since 1982. While players from other countries shake and shudder to think about that 12 yard kick, the German players exude confidence. Whether a national trait, or something more personal to the team set up, the players seem able to run with the pressure. They are able to cope.

They are able to cope because they embrace the discipline of Nervenstaerke – a German term for 'strength of nerves'. They feel fear in tight situations like everyone else but they manage the thoughts that can accompany anxiety during pressure play. Their physiology stabilises whilst others' race. Their mind remains clear whilst others' fog.

I want this for you and I want more for you.

I want Nervenstaerke from the first minute to the last minute. I want Nervenstaerke across the pitch from goalkeeper to striker. I want you to build a game that acknowledges the pressure, identifies its presence, and which delivers in the face of it and in spite of it.

- *Feel the pressure? Play on...*
- *Feel the pressure? Focus...*
- *Feel the pressure? Act with confidence...*
- *Feel the pressure? Manage yourself...*
- *Feel the pressure? Play front foot...*

Managing Yourself

Let's make this simple and not so unobtainable. Nervenstaerke is about managing yourself. It's not some mystical, magical trait that German footballers possess. Everyone can play with Nervenstaerke.

Champions from every sport learn the ability to play under pressure. They don't necessarily improve their performance as the heat builds, but they do maintain the same standards they demand from themselves in every game throughout.

And that is all it takes.

A footballer has to develop habits and patterns before and during a match that will help him be the very best he can be, irrespective of the burden of pressure he feels.

No matter what your ability with the ball, to play Nervenstaerke you just have to do the right things at the right time. You have to manage your thoughts, your feelings and your behaviours, actions and attitudes. That is all. And, somewhat paradoxically, it starts by exploring the negative.

Start with the Negative

"What is the very worst that is going to happen?"

This is a great question to ask yourself before you enter a high pressure situation. By asking it, you give your emotional brain an opportunity to cool and your nervous system a chance to calm.

So the worst that is going to happen is that you play badly – you miss some chances to score or you concede a soft goal. Your team may even lose. And of course you're going to be disappointed about this, and you may be annoyed, angry or frustrated. This is normal and this is to be expected. But those feelings of loss will settle and eventually disappear. "This isn't so bad. It's not life ending."

By thinking, briefly, about the impact of failure you can start to rationalise the feelings of anxiety you may experience before you play. Nobody likes to fail but, when it comes to soccer, every player will suffer losses; that is a definite. That is the nature of competitive sport, not just football. Sport is about dealing with disappointments. Losses happen, you cannot control them, but what you *can* control is your response to them. You must be ready to quickly accept the disappointment and move on.

The next time you are heading into a big game and feel your stomach start to churn, and your heart rate begin to rise, I'd like you ask yourself, "What is the worst that can happen today?" Become acquainted with what failure might look like to you – what it might look like and how it might feel. Sure, the answer will probably involve some pretty rubbish feelings, but those feelings won't last.

Quieten your brain and nervous system by examining the true impact of failure. This is a really effective way to start dealing with pressure situations.

Process Control

You have rationalised winning and losing. Both happen and both need to be dealt with. Now it's time to focus your mind correctly.

The soccer player who spends too much time thinking about the things he can't control is the footballer who will become overwhelmed with nerves. You must place your attention on the things you *can* control.

This means you must spend the build up to a game concentrating on the process. Anxiety will kick in if you place too much emphasis on the outcome of the game or on your personal performance. Telling yourself that you have to win or that you have to be man of the match is your entry point to crushing nerves.

Stay cool, calm and collected. Be intelligent – remind yourself of what you are trying to achieve.

"All I can do is stick to my script today. All I can do is use my controllers to execute my script. All I can do is keep my energy bars filled. I can control these things."

That beating heart, the butterflies in the stomach, and the nagging of negative thoughts, lessen when a soccer player attends to the controllable factors. You will instantly start to manage your fear – unclogging your mind of doubts and worries and supercharging your body ready for kick off.

Stick to Your Routine

Champions deal in consistency. They direct their mind and body towards a regular and stable set of habits and patterns no matter what the game. Stick to the match routine we set up in chapter thirteen. You need it now more than ever.

Adhere to it. Bond to it. Be relentless with it.

On match day, I want you to wake up and relax. Do something to distract yourself. You might even incorporate a pre-routine set of habits. Get up early and go for a walk, grab the newspaper from the corner shop or make yourself breakfast. When you're a couple of hours out from kick-off get your Nervenstaerke mind into gear. Mentally rehearse your script – picture it in detail – then head out to warm up your body and mind.

Experiencing Nervenstaerke during the game requires settling your nerves *before* the game. Get your warm up bang on, by adhering to the advice on using your controllers and your script under the next two headings. They must be used intentionally, deliberately, and with the purpose of getting you physically and mentally ready to play.

Use Your Controllers

When you take to the pitch, use your controllers. You have learnt to relax before the game; now, as you grace centre stage be demanding of yourself.

Use your self-talk controller to do so. Demand focus. Demand correct intensity. Demand assertiveness. Demand lively and strong and sharp – razor-sharp.

Support your inner voice by using your body controller. Get on your toes and start moving. Act free and loose and confident and big and brave.

Act free and loose and confident and big and brave. What does this look like? What does this feel like?

Stand tall. In the face of pressure, when the nerves are searing through your body, stand tall and proud. Use positive gestures. Dampen any nervous feelings that can suppress your game as quickly as you can by freeing up your body.

The combination of your two controllers can be an incredibly powerful way to get the very most from your pressure play.

If you're walking towards the penalty spot, affirm in your mind (using your self-talk) what you are trying to achieve. "I'm trying to score. I'm going to pick a spot to aim at. I'm going to strike the ball cleanly." Walk tall and upright. Place the ball on the spot with authority, decisively and with confidence. Start your run up with a single focus – getting a great strike on the ball and directing it towards your target.

Your controllers can help you score that winning penalty. They can help you stay calm when the heat is on.

Stick to Your Script

Remind yourself of your script and become it. To deal with the pressure he faces on a weekly basis, in the EPL, Yannick Bolasie will immerse himself in his BLR Ronaldo script, and all the plays and moves that go with it.

So much of coping with pressure is your ability to focus on the right things – specifically the process of play. Players who become overly anxious are ones who tend to orientate towards the score, the possible end result, and the evolving performance.

- *"I can't control the score so forget it, just stick to my script"*
- *"I can't force a great performance so forget it, just stick to my script"*

The script is about you and you alone. It can be controlled. If you find yourself dwelling on the things that take you away from your script, shift back instantly. Nervenstaerke requires a mind that, when playing in conscious mode, is fully immersed in the script. Not the outcome and not the performance. These just create unhelpful thoughts – they create ANTs

Squash the Killer ANTs

Scatter the ANTs as they hit you. They will come, they will be there, and your job is to deal with them ruthlessly.

When you hear an ANT, shift quick. Shift without delay. Shift by using your controllers to return to your script. Pressure hates a mindset that is nimble and flexible, one that can alter quickly.

Pressure can provide an infestation of ANTs. Accept this, it's the same for everyone. The footballers who are able to compete with Nervenstaerke are the ones who turn down the volume of ANTs by effectively using their controllers and by sticking to their match scripts.

They are the ones who meet ANTs with fun, freedom and focus. They play fearlessly. They play with expression when all those around them feel suppressed. They don't hide, they show. They play front foot football.

Commit to Front Foot Football

I'd like you to think about the most pressure-filled game of soccer you've been involved in or perhaps one that you've witnessed. Take a few moments to think about the behaviours of those players in the match. I think what you'll find is that those players who are overcome by nerves show it. It can be subtle and not always easily exposed, but there are definitely changes in performance.

You see players hiding. You see players who are less decisive, who are slower, and may have tunnel vision. They are crippled by fear and their awareness reduces… they don't see the 360 degree picture around them. They are slower to anticipate and muddled with their decision making. They can find themselves in the wrong position. They don't find space as easily and their movement is stilted and stuttering.

Nervenstaerke is the opposite. No matter what your nerves, play to win and not to avoid losing. Play with freedom and not with fear. Play on the front foot and not the back foot.

Accept your nerves and play with pace, play with power, play with perseverance.

Accept your nerves and play with commitment, play with confidence, play with control.

Accept your nerves and play with dedication, play with desire, play with discipline.

Technique Number 17
Under pressure, play with Nervenstaerke.

Perform Pep Talk

How you behave, and subsequently perform on the pitch, is dominated by the hormones you release inside of you. Your inside drives your outside!

I want you to relax before you compete. Too many soccer players become agitated, tight and tense before kick-off. I want you to be calm and clear. I want you cool and collected.

Now you're relaxed, I want you to start building that winning feeling. How? You need a matchday routine. You need a reliable set of procedures that help you get into the right frame of mind.

Start by picturing a successful script. Then rev up the intensity of your preparations by using your controllers during your warm up. Get on your toes and become alert, alive and lively. Get your head up, open your eyes and vocalise what you see on the pitch. Make your physical warm up a mental warm up.

Create a match day routine, and make it routine!

*

I want you to be passionate about the sentences and words you use as you play. They help you pay attention. They help you stay alert, alive and lively.

They also help you squash the bugs that infest your soccer brain – ANTs. Automatic Negative Thoughts are silent assassins in the world of football. They de-energise and distract. They sap confidence and arrest the physical, tactical and technical sides of your game.

ANTs need to be squashed. You need to SPOT, STOP and SHIFT the ANTs. You need to SHIFT with speed, without hesitation, so you avoid an infestation of those creepy crawlies.

Squash ANTs with speed.

When you play, I want you to play in the style of your script. I want you to use your two controllers to act out your script. I want you to use your self-talk and your body actions to keep your confidence bar full and maintain your energy bar as best you can.

I also want you to play with fun, freedom and focus. I talk with all my clients about these three F's, and I try to help them get the perfect balance between freedom and focus as our relationship develops.

Play with fun – a smile on your face or a sense of excitement running through your body. Play with freedom – take risks like a champion. And play with focus – build that sense of discipline by sticking to your match script.

It really is that simple. Crank up the volume of fun and enjoy yourself. Be expressive and play with freedom. Focus your mind on your script, your bars and your controllers.

Execute your match script with fun, freedom and focus.

*

Your self-talk is different to your thinking. Your thoughts *happen* to you, whereas you *do* your self-talk.

This is an important difference. Champions are accomplished at talking to themselves as they compete. Their self-talk lengthens their stride, sustains their drive and reminds them of what's important.

Combine your body controller with your self-talk controller. Say and do as you compete. Say and do, say and do, say and do…

Use your self-talk in combination with your body controller to keep your energy and confidence bars high and to focus on your script

*

I want you to play unconsciously, 80% of the time. And I want you to play conscious football 20% of the time. I want you to strike a keen balance between your unconscious and conscious.

Soccer players who compete 100% unconsciously can make mistakes without ever realising it. They can be sloppy. They can lose personal battles time and time again without striving to do anything to change the situation.

To be able to stay in an unconscious mental state of 'look and do', and to get the very most out of this state, it's important to use your controllers to stay alert, alive and focused. It's important to be ready to bring out your self-talk and body controllers at will.

Play 80/20 – use your conscious mind to get the most out of your unconscious game.

*

Nervenstaerke equals 'strength of nerves'. I want Nervenstaerke under pressure.

I want Nervenstaerke from the first minute to the last minute. I want Nervenstaerke across the pitch from goalkeeper to striker. I want you to build a game that acknowledges the pressure, identifies its presence, and which delivers in the face of it and in spite of it.

To find your Nervenstaerke, I'd like you to rationalise winning and losing, stick to the process, immerse yourself in your script, use your controllers, squash those killer ANTs and play front foot football.

Under pressure, play with Nervenstaerke.

Progress – Introduction

Plateau is the enemy of *progress*. It's a position so many soccer players find themselves in. Their improvement slows. They stop getting better. Frustration sets in.

So what happens? They get stressed. And what do they do? They try harder. But trying harder can tighten your muscles and muddle your mind. So trying harder reinforces the plateau or even makes your performance worse.

Constant improvement as a footballer requires a blend of strategies to improve your skills, to take control on the pitch and to develop your soccer image. Through your training script, your intentional practice and the on-pitch self-control tools I have introduced you to, you now have the ability to grow your skills and execute them consistently under pressure. But the hungry footballer needs more. The hungry footballer *wants* more. This is where your soccer image comes in.

In Soccer Tough I introduced the reader to the concept of the soccer image. In this section of the book we are going to build on these techniques. How you see yourself as a soccer player, your subjective opinion of your game is like a magnet for your true ability. A footballer won't consistently play better than her soccer image.

I'd like all soccer players to get a measurement of their soccer image. I think knowing how you see yourself as a footballer is imperative to your progress. The first chapter of this section provides you with a handy measurement scale to get to know exactly where your soccer image lies. Now I want you to progress this and here is how:

- Know how to analyse a game effectively and know when to be tough on yourself without destroying your confidence
- Get yourself physically fit, because just as your mind affects your body so your body influences your mind
- Use your memory and imagination to bolster your soccer image
- Speak to yourself in a manner that helps you deal with tough times and continue to build a positive soccer image

There are so many ways to shape your soccer image. It may be invisible to others but it's the foundation of progress for you. You have to see yourself capable of getting where you want to go if you want to give yourself a chance to get there. We will start by measuring this most important of personal qualities.

18

Your One True Vision

My work as a sport psychologist isn't just with the elite. It's not just the household names who seek that extra few percent from their game. I spend a lot of time travelling Europe working with footballers who play at the lower levels of the game. Here in England, this would be at League One, League Two and Non-League level.

The one thing I find many of these players have in common is that the majority have the potential to play at a higher level. They almost all have what it takes to compete in bigger leagues than the ones they are currently in.

Most League Two players in England I've worked with, have the skill and ability to fit into a League One or a Championship team (England's second tier). Some even have the capability of progressing to the EPL.

And this is no different to what I've experienced working with professionals in Spain, France, Italy, Poland, Switzerland and Germany. Most players have the capacity to move up a level, two, or even three.

What is stopping them? What is holding them back?

Of course, there can be many factors but a common thread running through their underachievement is the image they have of themselves as a soccer player. Too many League Two players see themselves as League Two players, but no better. They don't see themselves as Championship players. They don't have that inner vision of themselves playing at that level. Similarly, many Championship players struggle to believe that they are capable of playing in the Premier League and Premier League players battle to convince themselves that they can make the step up to International standard. They'd love to represent their country but they just don't *believe* they have the game to do so.

This phenomenon isn't reserved for British or European soccer. It's a global challenge. I frequently work with young players in the U.S. and find the same debilitating soccer images there. Many of them have great ability – enough to win college scholarships on highly successful programmes. But during their first year on their college team they perhaps don't perform so well. They are slow to react to passes, their movement is sluggish, and their passing is inaccurate.

They haven't suddenly become poor players overnight. It's because they don't feel they belong there. They don't feel they're a college scholarship player. They have a poor soccer image and are subsequently lacking in performance confidence.

This happens frequently with good players who have won a big move to a club in the EPL. I've worked with many. One of my clients was a brilliant striker in the English Championship. He set the pitch alight with dazzling displays and an incredible goal scoring record. It looked inevitable that he would transfer the skills he had shown to any club, on any pitch, anywhere in the World.

But when he arrived at his new club there were some really big names there. Players this footballer had always dreamed of playing with. Training suddenly felt a little daunting. He didn't want to make mistakes, and if he did he thought he'd look stupid. He believed that these players never lost or gave the ball away. They never missed great chances so he had to be equally perfect.

Similarly, come match day he felt intimidated. Was he really good enough to play on the same pitch as these players? He wasn't sure, and this apprehensive approach meant that his performances were reserved and shy. They were timid and fearful.

When he sat down and spoke to me about how he felt, it was clear that he had a Soccer Image problem. He had the ability to play top flight soccer. He had the hunger and commitment to do well at one of the biggest clubs in the world. The challenge that faced him was that he didn't see himself as one of the best soccer players in the country. He didn't *feel* like he belonged on the same team as his team mates.

It didn't matter that he had been knocking in goals from everywhere when playing for his Championship club. This was the Premier League and his brain wasn't allowing him to feel comfortable in his new environment. His brain was stopping him from seeing himself as an EPL footballer.

So we set to work, and the first thing we did was to put him on his Soccer Image Scale.

The Soccer Image Scale

After the striker and I had talked a little about the challenges he was facing, I asked him how good he thought he was as a soccer player in terms of ability. To help bring this alive I presented him with a scale of 1-100.

100 for this player represented a soccer image of being one of the top 10 players in the world. 10 for the striker was Sunday league amateur football. We built the picture of the scale further. 90 became the image of someone deemed as a world class player, while 80 became the image of an international striker. 70 was defined as the self-image of a Premiership striker, and 60 was marked as a Championship striker. 50 was ascribed for a League One footballer, while 40 was allotted as a League Two soccer player.

Almost instantly, my new client said he was at 78.

"I know I'm a Premiership footballer. I know I'm good enough. I'm happy to accept that I'm not one of the best Premier strikers out there and I don't feel I'm ready to win an international cap, I'm not at 80 yet – but I'm not far away."

Then we started to talk about his soccer image. I told him that his soccer image was something housed in the privacy of his mind. I told him that his soccer image was his true vision of himself as a player and it could only be evaluated by him. I said that the gauge most appropriate for measuring his soccer image was his feelings of comfort in the environment he was training and playing in.

Your soccer image is best measured by the feelings of comfort you experience in your training and playing environment.

I asked him to think about how comfortable he felt at his Championship club. I asked him to use his memory to think back to how he felt in each and every training session, and how he felt when he played at the level of Championship soccer.

"I felt really comfortable. I felt like I could score all the time. I felt like I was the best player at the club."

Then I asked him the same question but this time he had to judge his feelings of comfort at his new Premier League club.

"I definitely don't feel comfortable. In fact, I look around and feel very uncomfortable. I mean, there's all these great players here. I don't feel like I belong."

Bingo! This was great feedback. I told him that it was great that he felt that he was a Premiership player, that he gave himself 78. I confirmed that I had no doubts that he was that good. But then I asked him to rate his soccer image by really focussing on his brain's true vision of how good he thought he was. He was to base it on the comfort levels he felt in the different environments he had played in. He answered quickly.

"I think I'm at 78, but actually my soccer image is only about 68. I felt really comfortable at my Championship club but I've arrived at this level and I don't feel comfortable at all. I'm definitely not past that 70 mark."

Intellectually, this footballer knew that he was a really good player. The pundits and the fans supported this view as well. And the statistics backed it up too. But, emotionally, this soccer player wasn't at the same level as his actual ability. There was a sizeable gap between where he consciously thought he was and where he unconsciously was.

"You have the ability of 78 that is without doubt" I told him. "But your soccer image is at 68. Deep down you see yourself as a Championship player and it's holding you back. That is your true vision of yourself as a footballer. We have some work to do. We now have to bring your 68 up to a 78. And then we have to work on improving that 78 day by day, week by week, month by month, and season by season."

Your Soccer Image Scale

Where are you on your soccer image scale?

I ask this knowing that your scale will most likely be very different to the striker I've talked about above. Your 100 might not be the world's top 10 players but the best players in a league or two above you. It might be the best players in the NCAA College system.

Similarly, scales of 90, 80 and 70 will be different. They will probably refer to a certain level in your league structure. I can't tell you what your scale will look like, and what the different numbers will represent, but I urge you to try this task.

Start by marking yourself out of 100 (or out of 10 if you prefer) for your ability. How good do you think you are? Next, ask yourself how comfortable you feel at the level you're playing at. To reinforce this, tap into your memory. When you've played at lower levels have you felt very comfortable? At what level did things start to feel uncomfortable? Now use your imagination. If you competed for a team a level up would you feel comfortable and at ease around the other players? How far up in your league structure can you go until you think you'd start feel a little discomfort (when players would intimidate you and when you'd be overcome with nerves come match day)?

How do you see yourself as a soccer player? How would you describe yourself? What inner movie do you run when you take time to think about your game?

Many players who do this exercise with me are higher in their estimation of their ability than for their soccer image. They need to work on their soccer image and they do so by employing the tools and techniques I am going to talk about in the rest of this section.

The majority of players however, have them at about even. Their ability matches their self-image. These players have a firm grasp of their soccer consciously and unconsciously. They now need to work predominantly on their training scripts to improve their game, as well as introduce better preparation and improved performance protocols in order to enhance their ability score on the scale. If this is you, I still want you to incorporate the techniques from this section of the book so your soccer image keeps pace with your ability. This section isn't irrelevant for you as it involves further development of your ability and your soccer image.

There are some, albeit a small few, who mark themselves lower for ability than they do for their soccer image. Whether it's a personality trait, mental toughness or some other innate or learnt characteristic these players wouldn't feel out of place training and playing with footballers who are better than them. And that's great! Keep doing whatever you're doing to help your soccer image be that way. But now, let's get your game better. Let's set out a training script, a match script and keep building your soccer image alongside your ability.

Technique Number 18

Scale your Soccer Image.

19

Going Dark and Being Tough

Champions tend to be champions because they are tough on themselves. They have an inner voice aligned with excellence and they demand lung busting, effortful activity week in week out. This is how they grow as people and this is how they evolve as sporting competitors.

But the psychology of elite sport works in a subtle way. Just as you can't run around like a headless chicken on a soccer pitch, you can't constantly beat yourself up. Doing so leads to a mental agoraphobia that restricts freedom, imagination, confidence and focus.

The champion's mindset is flexible. The champion knows when to be tough and when to relax. The champion knows when to self-correct and when to self-praise. The champion develops the capacity to compartmentalise his or her thinking related to skills, strengths, weaknesses, and a desired future game.

This form of self-analysis is crucial to your ability to build the kind of soccer image that will help you progress your game and deliver high performances time and again.

To develop your image of your game, and to feel good come match day, you have to know when to be tough on yourself. You have to know when to turn up the volume of your self-criticism. Here's my guide to this most crucial of thinking skills.

Going Dark

You've played. The match is over and emotion swirls around your mind and impinges on every part of your body. Maybe it's been a great game, you've won and that emotion is elation. High fives and knowing smiles shared between team mates. Or maybe you've lost and that emotion, that feeling, is despondency.

Whether you are up or down, after a game, give yourself some time to let the outcome of the game sink in. No doubt, your coach will have a few things to say and some of your team mates will express their thoughts. Listen and absorb. Respect their analysis no matter how it is conveyed.

About an hour to two after the match, I want you to go dark. By this, I mean I want you to drain all the emotion from the game, and I want you to quieten your mind – now you're going to analyse your game.

To do this, take a few deep breaths and relax your muscles. Really focus on your breathing, your chest expanding and contracting. Pay attention to each breath and start to count them. By doing this, you are shifting your focus away from the emotion that you've felt for the past 30 to 60 minutes as a consequence of the game.

Tough on Process

Most soccer players are tough on themselves in the wrong way when it comes to matchday. They are tough on result and outcome. They are tough on performance. But, as has been the message throughout this book, the result is not something that is controllable and personal performance cannot be forced nor guaranteed.

I like footballers to be tough on process as they compete and analytically tough on process following the game. This is the area they should demand most from themselves. With that in mind, here is the first question you ask yourself when going dark – "What mark can I give myself out of 10 for my script?"

Follow this by asking yourself – "Did I use my controllers often enough? How successful was I at squashing ANTs? Did I keep my energy and confidence bars full?"

Take your time and be honest with yourself. If you didn't use your controllers… why not? Your self-talk and your body actions should be available to you all the time. You can choose to stay on your toes and alert, ready to receive the ball. If you weren't, then why not? You can choose to speak to yourself confidently no matter the score, no matter who the opposition are, and no matter your personal performance. If you let the ANTs engulf you, you need to ask yourself *why*. You need to be brutal with yourself.

My clients get to know very quickly that I want them to stretch themselves with their process. It is simply unacceptable not to be engaged in the script. If their bars get too low then they need to be a whole heap better at keeping them high and I tell them so.

If you can't give yourself, at the very worst, 8/10 for your script then you need to demand more from yourself. And remember, this isn't the same as performance. I'd never demand a great performance from anyone, but I certainly want a great process.

If the process has been poor then it's time to review the relevant chapters in this book and commit more resources to your processes during your training (perhaps your training script needs to shift more towards using your controllers and executing your match script?)

Don't rush your analysis of the process. Champions control the controllables. The more you take time to think about using your controllers, and being into the script, the better you'll become at using them. Your performances will then take care of themselves.

Performance Second

Now it's time to start building a highlights reel of your performance in your mind. This inner footage has to be balanced neatly between clips that help you feel good about yourself as a soccer player, and shots that will help you improve your game. Both work towards developing your soccer image.

Notice that I've used the term 'help you build your game'. Champions use poor in-game moments and instances of failure to fuel the fire of improvement. They treat them as sources of feedback for what needs to be better.

Soccer players who ignore the negatives after a game, lose no matter what. They lose because they won't learn from their mistakes. They won't get better.

Ask yourself this: "What is my mark out of 10 for today's performance?" You've asked the same question about your process, now is the time to break down your performance.

If you've given yourself a 6, I'd like you to ask yourself this: "Why as high as 6? What went so well that I've given myself as high a mark as 6?"

In this way, you get a chance to think about what was good. Even the worst performances should elicit two or three stellar moments. Even your 3/10 will provide moments of excellence. If you've been at your worst, acknowledge this, but while you go dark you are obliged to pick things that went well for you. You need these moments of mastery to feed your soccer image.

Next I'd like you to ask yourself: "I've given myself a 6 (as an example). What do I need to do to perform at a 7 or 8 next time?"

Champions enjoy this question because it's demanding. It offers a glimpse at what better looks like. You were at 6 in this game, so what does 8 look like? What does 9 look like?

If you can't personally observe excellence, even if only through your imagination, then you can't perform excellently. The information you collect by examining better must be considered with the next question: "Is there anything from this game I need to think about adding into my training script?"

If there are performance leakages that you think require being added to your training script then I'd be cautious about including them straightaway. If you do, you might find the training script becoming too bulky and unmanageable. By working on too many things in your practice sessions you'll halt your progression. Write down the performance area you feel needs serious attention and choose to include it in your script the following month.

Leaving Dark

Take some deep breaths again and relax. Shut your eyes if you want and stay still. You've been dark and you've analysed your game.

The emotion may rush back into your conscious awareness. That's okay. Football is an emotional game! You've now completed the task of self-analysis. You've been tough on yourself *in the right way* – you've built evidence for your soccer image, positive feelings that build your inner library of distinction. You've also found evidence for the improvements you need to make. This makes you a relentless footballer. It makes you an intelligent soccer player. Combined they make a lethal combination.

Tough on Training

If post-match self-analysis is a keen mix that examines the good and the bad, then your training thoughts should head predominantly in one direction.

Be tough on yourself in training. Be tough on yourself in training because, as was discussed in section one of this book, training is reserved for your zone of stretch.

Was I focused on my training script? Did I come out of my comfort zone? Was I better than yesterday?

Now let me be clear what I mean by 'tough on training'. You're going to get things wrong in an atmosphere of stretch so don't worry about mistakes. The manner I want you to be tough on yourself is whether you explored the zone of discomfort or not. If you did not then you're not trying hard enough. You're not fully embracing getting better.

Post training, start by asking yourself what went well. Always begin with the positive. But I really want you to turn up the volume of your critical voice when it comes to what should have gone better. I really want you to be your toughest critic of your training mentality, your training attitude and your training capability.

In training, you live outside of comfort. You practice on the edge. You dare to give the ball away; you dare to do things quicker, stronger, sharper and with greater versatility. When you reflect back on the hour or two you've trained, have you done this? Did you improve? Are you better than you were a few hours before?

Being tough on training requires a mindset that's attuned to pitch perfect. Perfectionism can be crippling on a matchday but in training it can be a fundamental for progressive practice. Be the details footballer – be the one who says "Not good enough" more often than not.

To improve your soccer image you have to develop skill. You have to develop every aspect of your game. So your soccer image is built from the stretch mentality I want you to foster in training.

Be tough on training.

Tough on Championship habits

Toughness on championship habits must be like the commitment you display towards brushing your teeth or having a shower. No one would contest that these habits of hygiene are anything but vital daily activities. For champions, great habits are like sticking to a strict diet and exercise regime – they may be a struggle to do at times but if you want success you're going to have to do them. You're going to have to execute them.

I've worked with many players who say to me that they want success. They envision the kind of footballing future they desire and they fall in love with the image and all that goes with it. They are motivated! But most of them aren't *committed* – there is a big difference between being motivated and being committed.

Motivation is fleeting. It comes and goes like the tides of the sea. Maybe you've watched an inspirational speaker on YouTube and you're now ready to take on the world. With music blaring you go to training. You train hard. You run, you jump, you lift. But you wake up the next day and you feel stiff and tired. You project your mind forward to the tiring exercises you have to complete and it exhausts you just imagining them. This is what motivation looks like. It's all too brief.

Commitment, on the other hand, is an everyday thing. It's an every week thing and an every month thing. It feels exhaustion but carries on regardless. It takes note of boredom but continues no matter what.

Performance profiling, video analysis, that extra rep, the last lung busting five minutes of a game, failure, mistakes, muscles that burn, that extra step, visualising, on your toes non-stop, getting to bed early, cognitive overload. The greats execute great habits. They commit daily, hourly, minute-by-minute to these habits.

My concern is that so many players are motivated... but they're not always committed. They want to do well, boy they want to do well. They want to play first team college soccer. They want to stay in the team. They want their team to be a Championship winning one. And maybe they're eager – they want more. They want to play MLS. Perhaps they want to go even further. They want to go to Europe to play the EPL, La Liga, Serie A or Bundesliga.

I say to them – just as I say to my players – it's great to be motivated, but it's imperative to always be committed! Commit to the everyday habits and patterns that engage your mind and body and which produce championship winning form.

Of course, commitment can be dull and boring and sweaty and gut wrenching. It doesn't always look attractive. It doesn't always look fun and it doesn't always look cool. You have to be different, you can't be a sheep. You have to be tough – tough on yourself to do the things that are going to help you go where you want to go.

When you think "I can't be bothered" that's an ANT. Define it as such. Declare it as an automatic negative thought.

When you think "I'll leave it until later" that's an ANT, squash it and do it now!

When you feel lethargic and are tempted to skip a set, this is an ANT. SHIFT to a 'can do' determined attitude.

Commitment starts with defining precisely what it is you have to do on a daily basis and then doing these precious actions and behaviours. It is followed through by classifying those thoughts that prevent you from completing important habits as ANTs.

Those thoughts, those ANTs, can also come as feelings. They may not be thoughts in your head, they may come as destructive feelings such as lethargy, despondency, tiredness, boredom or sluggishness. These may be feelings but to me they are also ANTs. They must be overcome and you must execute the actions you have scheduled for yourself with an accompanying attitude of energy and focus.

Complete the set, finish the run, be thorough, do it in full. Never cut corners, never be half-hearted and never give in to the ANTs. Committing to doing this will help you explore just how good you can become.

Technique Number 19

Be Tough on Yourself.

20

The Body That Rayan Builds

"Not one player has a slow start to the season."

Ray tells me this with a determined look on his face. "They all come flying out of the blocks: hungry, ready. Why wouldn't they feel that way – they've gone on vacation for a couple of weeks, recharged the batteries, and then they've dedicated themselves to a committed two to four weeks of intense training. They're one step ahead of everyone else. They're on fire before everyone has even thought about pre-season training."

I'm in Bristol, England, for the Back2Action training camp that Premier League strength and conditioning coach Rayan Wilson organises for elite and elite-in-waiting players over the month of June. Ray is slowly building a reputation for helping some of the finest and brightest young players improve beyond expectation. He does this by helping them construct a body that moves faster, works harder, and functions better.

June is the quiet time for English football. It's the off-season and most players are sunning themselves on the beaches of Europe, but Ray's footballers are working to prepare themselves for their best season ever. They're working on their technical skills, they're honing their mentality and they're becoming fitter and stronger.

A small-sided game is taking place and there's a heady mix of talent on display. A few Premier League players, four or five from the English Championship, and the rest from the lower leagues. One touch passing, fast feet, playing head up to improve awareness – ambitious players doing overtime while others rest on their sun loungers.

Ray looks on, an eye for detail, as single-minded as his players. He's looking at movement and at bodily form, the small actions that show any physical impairments from the players. It is in the game itself that Ray tries to spot the deficiencies that hold players back and cause injuries. Just as I am passionate about the soccer mindset, Ray is passionate about the footballing body. But we both know that mind and body are integrated.

In many ways, my work helps to improve the functioning of the bodies of players. By managing their mindset and mentality on and off the pitch, they can become more aware of their team mates and the opposition on the pitch, they can anticipate quicker and demonstrate greater flexibility in their decision making. By focusing their minds, they can push themselves to run for longer and they can exert more energy in the dying minutes of a game.

Just as mind influences body so body influences mind, and Ray is so much more than a physical trainer. His work cleanses the brain, un-fogs the mind and improves clarity of thought. By helping players be all they can physically be, he opens the door for the kind of mental consistency that a footballer needs.

I work the mind and impact the body. Ray works the body and impacts the mind. This incredibly powerful combination is something every prospective soccer player should seek out. And one footballer who is exposed to this formidable formula is Yannick Bolasie, BLR Ronaldo.

The Story of Ray and Yannick

Ray is the most important coach in Yannick Bolasie's life. He's there for him daily and he's shaped a physical regime that is truly helping Yannick discover just how good he can be.

Yannick met Ray when playing for Bristol City in the lower league of English football. He told Ray he yearned for more and Ray was more than happy to oblige. And so Ray and Yannick put their heads together and constructed a gruelling programme of physical training to complement the regime Bolasie was getting from his club. Here are some examples of the work they've done together.

Focus

When defender Branislav Ivanovic knocked Yannick off the pitch into the stands during a Chelsea v Crystal Palace match, Bolasie realised he had to work on his strength and balance. As a winger, he couldn't afford to be bullied. He couldn't allow himself to be pushed off the ball.

The sense of humiliation Yannick felt at incidents like this, combined with the knowledge that he had to be in the best physical shape he could possibly be to discover his true potential, led him to work diligently with Ray Wilson several times a week.

If you get the opportunity to sit down with Yannick and discuss his physical preparation he will explain to you that he works on his footballing body because he wants his soccer brain to improve.

Yannick understands that moments when a footballer gets out-muscled or beaten to the ball are hazardous to a player's confidence. When Chelsea defender Ivanovic pushed Bolasie around, he lost focus. Doubts started creeping in and he began to believe he wasn't physically equipped to play in the Premier League.

Yannick is right about the link between mind and body. Too often, I hear players tell me they switched off because they started to lose the physical battle. Their concentration was compromised as a result of the powerful play of the opposition.

Of course, I work with these players to improve their ability to use their controllers – their self-talk and their body actions. I ask them to have their script at the forefront of their minds so they can re-focus back onto the present quickly and quietly. But I also discuss with them the link between body and mind. By being physically equipped, they can become mentally tough.

One very important area of mental toughness is the ability to focus. When a player is strong and powerful, he increases his chances of winning the physical battle and subsequently lessens the risk of being distracted. This is what Yannick has found. His work with Ray has allowed him to win more personal battles and as a consequence he's been less distracted.

Whenever Yannick lines up for a Premier League game, he knows he's playing in one of the physically toughest leagues in the world. But this is no longer an issue for him. He has trained his body and by doing so, he has developed his focus. He is now less likely to get pushed off the pitch. He can unconsciously let his body do its thing and focus his mind fully on the responsibilities within his role. He can get on with his job.

Inner Pictures

"I want you to get this right,. I want you to drive your foot into the floor. Then I want you to imagine your feet are hitting hot coals, too hot to touch for any period of time – create power in your legs and speed in your feet...

...Okay, do it again, do it with precision. Picture those hot coals, think about it, do it with precision...

...And again, and again, do it with precision, drive down to the hot coals then up quickly, quicker, with extreme speed – with precision."

Ray's training enhances Yannick's imagery and visualisation. The pictures he asks Yannick to envision initiate physical excellence. They fire his imagination and creativity.

Picture your legs driving into hot coals rising up quickly because of the unbearable heat of the coals. Use this image to increase power and speed.

A renowned athletic trainer once told me that he felt the Brazilian soccer players were so good at football because of their love of Capoeira. This martial art combines dancing and acrobatics and is something most young Brazilians grow up practicing. They learn to throw body shapes then they learn to kick a ball. In this way they become more skilful. They improve their ability to stay balanced and they improve their capability to take on players and go around them.

The combination of movement and strength training is something that Ray emphasises to Yannick. He feels the ideal soccer body can shift and shape as well as act as a battering ram.

And when you see Yannick Bolasie play soccer, you see a body at play. You see it turn and twist, as much as you see speed, strength and stamina. And Yannick visualises this daily. He sees the plays he wants to make Monday through Friday so when Saturday comes – his body is primed for action. He has the confidence to play.

Yannick is a keen collector of inner pictures of excellence. He can imagine – in detail – his body winding around defenders, his legs pumping with vigour, and his feet dancing with the delight and excitement that you get when you're playing the game you love the most.

I'd like you to picture your physicality and athleticism. I'd like you to see yourself jump and run and tackle and shoot. Make your personal movie detailed – the better you see, the more the brain actually thinks it's happening. The more your brain believes it, the more imaginative you can become.

Fire your imagination, daily. Relate your catalogue of pictures to the work you are doing now with your physical self. The more you do this, the more creative you can become and the more confidently you can play.

Bodily Confidence and the Confidence to Play

When Yannick walks out of the tunnel every week onto some of the most celebrated pitches in the world, in front of thousands and thousands of screaming fans, he knows that he's physically equipped to deal with whatever the opposition have in store for him.

He knows that he can win the battle of the body. He knows he won't be out-muscled. He knows he can leave a defender for dead. He knows he can get that extra yard and he knows his energy bars will last that bit longer.

He knows because he is diligent about his physical conditioning. And this diligence fuels his performance confidence. He feels great about his footballing body so he feels great about his game. Every week, he's ready to go. Every match, his body swirls with excellence.

On a Saturday, he can look back to a week of quality training. He can say, "I've worked hard and I've worked efficiently. I'm ready physically and this helps me feel ready mentally."

He is ready physically so he can be ready mentally.

The sessions he does with Ray during the week help him to sizzle on Saturday – a crackling confidence that's infectious. He sprays it on his team mates when they see his positive body language and upbeat attitude. They see his athleticism, they see his dynamism, they see his movement and they grow in confidence themselves. The strikers know they will get crosses delivered to them. The midfielders know they will have someone to pass to. The defenders know he will be quick to get back and cover defensively. The whole team knows he will work hard. Yannick's athleticism gives them peace of mind.

Are you working hard to develop your footballing body? Are you able to run onto the pitch and crackle with confidence because of the speed of your feet, the strength of your torso, and the endurance of your muscles?

If not, why not? If not, then you are missing out on an incredible confidence creator. If not, start building your physicality, at your endurance and at your athleticism.

Persistence

By working with Ray, Yannick has also improved his temperament. Ray is a details man, he doesn't do sloppy and he won't accept less than the best, most focused, exercises in the gym.

"One more set Yan, keep pushing, keep going"

"Strong, keep working, keep going, keep pushing, stay strong"

Ray trains Yannick Bolasie's persistence. He charges the batteries on his self-talk controller. He fires up his energy bar and gives him the mental tools to keep his bars high, no matter what.

Of course, there are times when Yannick finds the training a little tedious. All footballers feel this way from time to time. But Yannick just gets on with it. He doesn't stop. He doesn't give into the boredom. He keeps going – he completes the set, he completes the exercise, and he sees out the training session.

It is this commitment to excellence that separates players. It is this commitment to the discipline of great habits that sees you searching your bottomless pit of potential. It is your job to think and act like there are no limits to your ability – doing your physical work and completing your sets is a lethargy busting activity that is a non-negotiable for Yannick, and it should be for you too.

Finish the set and you'll run that extra yard on the pitch. Start your exercises early and you'll play a better first five minutes. Stretch your body more and you'll stretch your ability to win the ball back.

"Stay strong, keep moving, keep working, complete the set, stretch further"

The soccer athlete is not only more persistent, she can be a different beast. She sees a different, better game because the work she does on her football body helps improve her soccer image.

Improving your Soccer Image

- *"I'm fit, really fit. I'm ready to use my fitness to work harder than ever"*
- *"I'm working on my strength and I feel super strong. I can use this strength to win my aerial battles and win my one-on-one challenges."*
- *"I'm ready to run further than I ever have before"*

Is there a better tonic for your soccer image? Combined with your memory and imagination exercises, working on your athleticism and physicality is one of the most effective ways to change how you see yourself as a soccer player.

- *"I will use my speed to be first"*
- *"I will use my new strength to be stronger in the challenge"*
- *"My new pace can leave others behind"*
- *"My shots are powerful"*

Who are you as a footballer? How would you feel on the training pitch with players a league above you? An age group older than you?

You can work towards feeling technically as good. You can make the effort to become mentally as equipped. So why not push towards being physically and athletically as competent? Combining these three will supercharge your soccer image. You will upgrade how you feel about yourself as a footballer.

Work technically, work mentally, and work physically. Become Soccer Tough in the gym. Lift the weights and complete the sets. Eat well and sleep soundly. You have a bottomless pit of potential and if you want to discover just how deep that potential is then you simply have no other option.

No Other Option

If you're not working on yourself physically then you're not working to be the very best you can be. You don't have a bottomless pit of potential. You are limiting yourself.

If you're not working on yourself physically then you're not getting the most from your mindset and mentality. You're missing out on incredibly powerful opportunities to work on your focus, to improve your ability to visualise, and to enhance your persistence. You're missing out on sessions that train your confidence.

If you're not working on yourself physically then you're not building the kind of soccer image that makes champion footballers.

This to me is unacceptable. I want you *knowing* that you've done all you can to be fitter and quicker and stronger. I want you *knowing* that you've worked hard to be more agile, more robust and more resilient. I want you *knowing* that you'll run onto the pitch feeling great.

Physically proficient players make the game awkward for their opponents. They scare them. When Yannick picks up the ball on the wing, he wants the defender to feel fear. He wants the full-back to feel scared, not only by the skill in his feet but also by his physical presence.

- *"I can't show him down the line – he's too fast"*
- *"I can't close him down quickly – he's too strong!"*
- *"I can't show him inside – he's too confident"*

Can you see what Yannick's work with Ray has done? He's now so quick, so strong and so confident that he's scaring others! Sure, he brought a lot of skill to the table, but Yannick's work on his physicality has *accentuated* his skill. His physical presence plagues the mind of the opposition full backs. It strikes fear into their heart and doubt into their mind. For Yannick, himself, it has added a sense of certainty and assuredness.

- *"If I go down the line I can use my pace"*

- *"If he gets close to me I can use my strength"*
- *"If he shows me inside I'll take him on or spot my pass"*

By including a comprehensive programme of physical work to your repertoire of strengths, you too can play with this type of confidence.

It might be that most of you reading this will never be an English Premier League player but that's not the point. Who cares? By working on your mindset *and* your physicality you can become the very best you can be. You can trademark your personal brand of excellence. If that means team mates look on and shake their head at your extra stretching exercises then so be it. If it means you've got to put in a few more hours of effort a week then I reckon that feeling of dominance you'll get on the pitch when you play a match will more than make up for the added time.

By committing to improving your body, you pledge an allegiance to the winning habits that shape a soccer image made for distinction. I want this for you. I want you to be immersed in being quicker, being more powerful, and more agile. I want you to be committed to developing a stronger body as well as to building a body that's equipped to go the distance – and further!

Technique Number 20

Work on your physicality and your athleticism.

21

To Remember, To Dream

In Soccer Tough, I introduced the reader to the importance of memory and imagination in soccer. I want players to be able to remember themselves at their very best and I want them to spend time envisioning their dream game.

Three years on, and my work with footballers has moved forwards. I have spent time with some of the best players and coaches in the world. I have delivered at conferences and workshops across the globe. And I remain steadfast in my point of view – memory and imagination are the most important ingredients to your soccer image and subsequently to your ability to keep progressing.

By remembering your best, you keep feeding your brain the nourishment it needs to keep learning. Your very best games serve you pictures that help you feel good. When you feel good, your mind opens up to your learning environment.

What does your best game look like? What does it feel like?

And, by remembering your best games, you have an active template to perform highly and consistently time and time again. Etching it into the deeper parts of your brain will help your top performances become who you are as a soccer player. They will shape your soccer image.

"What does my best look like? What does my best feel like? I am alert, alive and lively. I am wide-eyed and aware. I see more and I do more. I feel strong, I feel relentless, I feel athletic and I feel energised. I am my very best game. This is who I am and this is what I do."

See this template time and time again: every day, every week, every month. Make it one of your daily habits and be tough on yourself to make sure you do it. This will ward off the plague of plateau. It will keep your mind and body pumping the feel good chemicals even when you have below average training sessions and performances.

In equal measure, I want you to become addicted to the look and feel of your dream games. What does 10/10 look like? What does 12/10 look like? What does 15/10 look like?

Explore the ridiculous! Mull over the game of the masters. Fixate your focus on the unrealistic. That's okay to do. Today's imagination is tomorrow's reality.

- *What does it look like to play like Messi? What does it feel like?*
- *What does it look like to play like Neuer? What does it feel like?*
- *What does it look like to play like Abby Wambach? What does it feel like?*
- *What does it look like to play like Asisat Oshoala? What does it feel like?*

Exercise your imagination daily. Support the physical work you're doing on your game by drilling your mind with hope and wonder and curiosity. It doesn't necessarily mean you can play like those players, but it does mean you are doing something practical to get as close to them as you possibly can.

You soccer game is your soccer brain. And you get to shape your soccer brain. You get to *choose* how it is shaped. You can carve it into a centre of excellence by providing it with the right inputs.

The right inputs include your training script. It includes your match script and it includes your controllers. By telling your brain that you are in charge on the practice pitch, and on matchday, then you are shaping a strong soccer image – one that affirms that you are in control.

Other inputs should include the memories of you at your best and the possibility of the future perfect.

- *What does my best game look like? What does my best game feel like?*
- *What will it look like if I play my dream game on Saturday? What will it feel like?*

Every input counts towards the quality of your soccer image. Inputs that are unhelpful and destructive, the ones that are ANTs, subtract from your image. They negatively affect confidence and, subsequently, performance.

Of course this doesn't mean you ignore your weaknesses. We discussed, in Section One, the importance of examining the areas of your game you feel you need to improve. Similarly, when you 'go dark' and analyse your performance after the match you need to explore what went wrong and what wasn't so good. Both of these 'negative' processes are important and they shouldn't be ignored. But they need to be compartmentalised. They need to be short, sharp examinations of your game. At all other times you need to dwell on your strengths, your best games and your dream games. Getting the balance right is crucial if you want to build your soccer image and your self-belief.

A Footballer....

A footballer who believes he has a bottomless pit of potential builds his soccer image. A footballer who goes dark, and analyses his game in the most appropriate manner, builds his soccer image. A footballer who is tough on himself in the right way builds his soccer image. Now, add the tools of memory and imagination to the list of strategies to help bolster your image on a day by day basis.

See the best of the past and predict the best of the future. When you do this, it becomes easier to deal with the challenges you face on and off the pitch. And this is something we're going to work on in our final chapter.

Technique Number 21

Remember to remember and dare to dream.

22

The Power of Yet!

There are two paths weaving their way into your footballing future.
Two paths that start with a subtle difference but gently widen further
apart. The horizon looks very different for these journeys.

Path one is the 'never' path. The 'never' path is the one that takes a
soccer player into the land of no improvement. And it's the path that
I'd guess every player takes at some point in their footballing career.

It's the destructive path. When you tread its turf, waves of frustration or
despondency can surge through your body.

- *"I'm never going to get this right"*
- *"I'm never going to get into this team"*
- *"I'm never going to be as good as her"*
- *"I'm never going to impress him"*
- *"I'm never going to master this skill"*
- *"I'm never going to be good enough for a scholarship"*

This path delivers doubt and fires anxiety. It stops you from carrying on
when it's imperative that you do so. It's the path that damages your
soccer image.

There is of course another path to take. This is the 'yet' path. It's the
path of champions.

- *"I haven't made the team... yet!"*
- *"This skill is tough to master. I haven't got it... yet!"*
- *"I'm not good enough for a scholarship... yet!"*

The 'yet' path is one of persistence and perseverance. It's the path to take if you really want to discover just how good you can be. It's the path that improves your soccer image.

'Yet' is a word I want you to say when you are working on your skills. I want you to incorporate it into your training script. I'd like you to adopt the attitude that there is no 'never' and no 'can't'. There is only can – you just haven't got there yet.

Remember, you have a bottomless pit of potential, and it is your job to think, to train, and to play like there is no limit to your ability. If you are finding certain skills tough to master, if you feel like giving up, then remind yourself of the power of yet. You just haven't mastered the skill, yet!

This is something that a client of mine has become brilliant at doing. My client, I'll call him Johnny for the purpose of this chapter, used to be a 'never' footballer. As an 18-year-old first year professional at a Premier League club he had displayed a lot of promise – these clubs don't give away professional contracts lightly. But being a first year pro is tough and by the time I'd met him, Johnny was finding it hard going.

Johnny had been one of the best players at the club's Academy, but as a first year pro, unless you are exceptional, you have to start again at the bottom rung of the professional ladder. Joining the development squad (18-21 years of age) he had to be focused and he had to exercise patience.

But finding the game easy as a teenager hadn't helped Johnny become the most patient of footballers. He was hungry for success and he wanted it straightaway. Midway through his first year in the pro ranks, he started to drop in form and fall away. Question marks had started to appear next to his name in his coaches' eyes. Was he really Premier League material? But this was nothing as compared to his own negative inner voice.

During our first session together, it was fairly obvious what we had to focus our work on. Johnny was very despondent and frequently referred to numerous doubts he had about his capability of playing at the very top level of soccer.

"I was so good at the Academy, but now I don't think I'm good enough to be in the Premiership. I don't think I am good enough to get into the first team. I'm never going to improve enough to be good enough to play Premier League football."

The curse of 'never' had hit Johnny hard.

The reality was that Johnny was still the talented young player that coaches had been excited about. And reports from the coaching staff suggested that Johnny was still demonstrating plenty of the skills required to play top flight football. But the environment he was training in was harder than he'd ever experienced… with players who were stronger, quicker, more athletic and technically superior. Johnny responded to this with a 'never' mindset:

- *"I will never be as good as them technically"*
- *"I will never be as strong as them"*
- *"I will never be as fast as them"*

Johnny had to change his language. He had to change his attitude towards the challenges he faced.

- *"I'm not as technically good as them… yet!"*
- *"I'm not as strong as them… yet!"*
- *"I'm not as fast as them… yet!"*

Johnny needed to develop an individual training script and accompany it with the word 'yet'. He needed the path of persistence and of perseverance. He needed to be disciplined and he needed commitment.

So we got to work. We agreed that the words 'never' and 'can't' were ANTs. Johnny decided that whenever he heard himself utter those words under his breath, he would squash them instantly by shifting towards a sentence that contained the word yet. "I'm not there yet" became his mantra.

- *"It wasn't my best training day today, I'm not there… yet!"*
- *"I made mistakes, but that's okay, I'm just not there… yet!"*
- *"I haven't been chosen for the first team… yet!"*

Of course it wasn't easy to change his 'never' mindset but soon Johnny learnt to love his training script. He enjoyed the challenge of working on the details of his game and he stopped becoming overemotional about mistakes and errors. And, as he learnt the power of 'yet', how he saw himself as a footballer began to change. His soccer image began to develop.

The Change that Yet Makes

When you start to banish 'never' from your soccer speak, and you begin to take the path of 'yet', so your soccer image starts to change.

It changes from 'can't do' to a 'can do'. It changes from destructive pessimism to energising optimism. It changes from a vision of bleak to a vision of peak.

When a soccer player says 'yet', they open up a window of opportunity. They get to express themselves rather than feel suppressed. They keep doing the same good things, and the same good habits, daily. They keep going, through failure, until they get to the place they want to be or as close to it as it's possible for them to get.

And this is a crucial point. Just because you keep making an effort to get where you want to be as a footballer, and just because you work your backside off, and you work smart, doesn't mean you are definitely going to achieve the very highest goals you set yourself.

You may not reach the first team. You may not win the title. You may never be man of the match. You may never score 20 goals in a season. But always *do the right things daily to give yourself the best opportunity to*. Always squash the ANT that is 'never', and always commit to 'yet'.

You don't know who Johnny is but he's going well. He's played for the first team and he enjoyed his debut. He played well and he battled hard using his match script and his controllers.

Every day, Johnny goes into training with his mind on 'yet'. And when he fails, which he does often, he utters the word 'yet' and reminds himself of another philosophy we've injected into his game. Johnny is big on mastery, and he TAPPs it every day.

TAPP Mastery

Things will go wrong. It's inevitable.

Goals will be scored against you. You'll be dropped. You'll be benched. Your team will go on a run of bad results. The coaching staff will display frustration towards you.

Things will go wrong. It's unavoidable.

You'll misplace passes and mistime tackles. You'll miss great chances and you'll concede a goal and it will be your fault. Your club will bring in a player with great ability who plays in your position and you'll turn up for matches and feel threatened.

Things will go wrong. But you have to deal with them. If you don't, you'll damage your soccer image. If you don't, you'll be wracked with doubt and worry. If you don't, your performances will be affected and your development will be stilted.

When I first start working with a player, I'm quick to tell them that I can't sprinkle magic dust on them. I let them know that there are no guarantees of success. But I let them know that whilst challenges will crop up, I will offer my support by helping them become passionate about mastery.

Mastery means to be skilful. It means to have control and to have the power to dominate and defeat setbacks. When you think of your soccer, I want you to be consumed by mastery. I want you to be impassioned about getting better – about learning, developing and improving. I want you to work towards dominating. I want you to work towards high skill. I want you to work towards being the very best you can be. And I want you to adopt this attitude irrespective of the trials and tribulations that you encounter within your game, at your club, within your squad and team, and with your coaches.

- *You get dropped – focus on mastery*
- *You lose a match – focus on mastery*
- *You make a couple of mistakes – focus on mastery*
- *You start on the bench – focus on mastery*
- *You have a bad training session – focus on mastery*

When you play competitive sport, and when you mentally sign up for the challenge of becoming a champion in a sport, then difficulties will arise. Every player is different in personality, temperament and personal characteristics, but a solution for everyone – during tough times – is to focus on mastery.

When 'stuff' happens, direct your brain towards mastery. Occupy your attention on what *you need to improve and what needs to get better*. Manage your thoughts by reminding yourself of your training script and your constant search for excellence.

It really is that simple. Just focus on getting better at your soccer when faced with adverse conditions or a run of poor form. And to help you get even better at being into mastery, I have a mantra that I ask players to repeat to themselves when they are striving to return to the state of mastery.

I want them to TAPP mastery. The 'T' stands for trust. The 'A' for accept. The 'P' represents patience, while process is the last 'P'. Let's look at them one at a time.

Trust

"I trust my ability. I trust what I bring to the field of play every day. I trust my improvement programme."

Great soccer players have a great amount of trust in themselves, in their everyday training, and in the matchday process they have put in place. They know that, given the right training script and the correct match script, they will continue to improve and to play with greater consistently.

During tough times, footballers need to turn up the volume of trust. They need to trust the everyday soccer tasks they set themselves.

"Stop stressing. I trust the work I am putting in. I trust that every second and every minute of what I do will take me where I want to go in this game."

Mastery is impossible without trust. If you can't trust yourself, and you can't trust the programme of improvement you have put in place, mastery isn't possible. It's impossible!

"It's okay, I made a mistake. I gave a goal away, but it's okay. I know my training script will cut down those errors. The coach isn't pleased with me right now but I just have to keep working on my script and focus."

Accept

Acceptance in football is essential. It's a forerunner to a relaxed mindset. By accepting that 'stuff' happens, you reduce stress and anxiety.

"I accept that 'stuff' will happen. I accept that part of soccer is to make mistakes. And I accept that being chosen for the team is out of my control. All I can do is keep striving to get better."

A soccer player must accept the challenges the brain delivers. Doing so cools the emotional part of the game. Instead of a sudden rush of negative emotion when something bad happens, an accepting footballer is able to react and respond effectively.

Trust and acceptance are a marriage made in heaven. Trusting your ability and accepting that your ability will be stretched – due to factors that are so often out of your control – helps you keep a rational, calm head.

"I trust and I accept. I trust the journey I am taking and I accept I will be tested. I will encounter problems, some of which will feel unfair. But that's okay, I accept that and I trust myself and my ability. I trust what I have put in place to become the best I can be."

Patience

Patience is a mental quality that a soccer player can never have too much of. And it's an attribute that needs work. Just as you lift weights, to get stronger, so you need to be patient to become more patient!

"Relax, calm... be patient. It's okay that 'stuff' has happened. I just have to be patient. I know I'm doing the right things. I can't force success. Success will come to me if I'm patient."

A lack of patience is accompanied by tight muscles. It leads to cortisol (your stress hormone) surging through your body, which prevents high performance. It also slows skill acquisition. You won't be a great learner when you act with impatience.

"Patience, I'll work hard to get back in the team. I can't force my way back in. Just be patient."

Being patient is a forerunner to being relaxed. Relaxation is a necessary ingredient if you want to improve. You'll never break into the team if you're tight and tense. You'll never score 20 plus goals as a striker if you're forcing your goal count. And you'll never keep clean sheets if you're stressing about trying to do so.

- *"Relax, calm... be patient. I'll score goals..."*
- *"Relax, calm... be patient. I'll keep clean sheets..."*
- *"I trust my ability. I accept the challenges and the bad times. I remain patient no matter what happens..."*

Practice

- *"I know where I want to get to. I've profiled the next level. I have a new training script. My script is by my bed – I wake up to my future game. It's written on my fridge – my mental nutrition reinforced daily. It's in my kit bag – it's the last thing I look at before I take to the pitch."*
- *"I commit myself to practice. I build race tracks in my brain – big, thick, speedy, powerful race tracks. Failure is inevitable but I'll continue to reach for Ronaldo and I'll continue to stretch for Smith."*

Because this is what winners do – winners envelope patience with practice. When failure strikes hard, they immerse themselves in getting better. Nothing and no-one holds them back.

Through adversity, champions trust their ability. They accept what has happened to them. They remind themselves that the journey is long and that they have to meet tough times with patience. And then they focus their mind fully on practice.

It's not because practice makes perfect or practice makes permanent. It's because practice distracts them from the problems that inevitably arise on their journey to excellence. It's because practice helps them focus their mind and dissolves the irrelevant stuff into the background. Trust, Accept, Patience, Practice. TAPP mastery.

"I want to get better and better and better. I want to improve my skills, my tactical knowledge, and my mindset. I want to execute my processes on the pitch as best I can."

Technique Number 22

Never say never, always say yet, and TAPP mastery.

Progress Pep Talk

You may *think* of yourself as being capable of performing at a certain level but you may not *feel* that you can. Your soccer image dominates your game, and this is the one true vision you have of yourself as a footballer. It's the vision that can hold you back or propel you.

Your soccer image is best measured by the *feelings* of comfort you experience in your training and playing environment. Measure how good you think you are on a scale of 0-100 as a soccer player and then measure your soccer image on the same scale.

When you feel uncomfortable in your soccer environment it means you are playing above the level of your soccer image. You are out of your comfort zone. These feelings might take the form of nerves, doubts or worries. They need to be managed and then you need to work on the image you have of yourself as a soccer player.

Scale your Soccer Image

*

Champions are tough on themselves in the right way. You may be a little scared to criticise your personal performances in matches but all the best sports competitors do. They just do so in the correct manner.

Firstly, be tough on your process. Did you use your controllers? Did you stick to your script? Did you squash ANTs? If not, why not? Now you've dealt with process, take some time to analyse your performance. Process first, performance second.

Champions are also tough on championship-winning habits. They repeat on a daily basis the actions that lead them towards excellence. They are motivated *and* they are committed. They leave no stone left unturned to be the very best they can be.

It is this toughness that helps them build their skills. It is this toughness that helps them build a winning mentality. And it is this toughness that helps them build their soccer image.

Be Tough on Yourself

*

Just as mind influences body, so body influences mind.

Working on your physicality cleanses the brain, un-fogs the mind, and improves clarity of thought. Improved athleticism opens the door to the kind of mental consistency that a footballer needs.

Do a work-out. A session working on your body trains the mind as well as the torso. You will improve your soccer image and you will believe in yourself more. You give yourself a better opportunity to accomplish more on the pitch.

Strong, powerful and endurance-filled soccer players focus better and are less easily distracted. They run onto the pitch with greater confidence, knowing that their bodily make-up helps them win challenges, reach for headers, pass more accurately, shoot more powerfully, see more and do more.

The message is simple – if you're not working on yourself physically then you're not working to be the very best you can be.

Work on your Physicality and your Athleticism

*

I want players to be able to remember themselves at their very best. I want them to recreate strengths, recall standout games and memorise match winning moments.

By remembering your best, you keep feeding your brain the nourishment it needs to keep learning. And by remembering your best games, you have an active template to perform highly and consistently, time and time again.

Alongside your work on your memory, exercise your imagination daily. Dare to dream of a game that is beyond your capabilities right now. Provide your nervous system with a template of the extraordinary.

By using your memory and imagination every day, you help yourself build a better, stronger soccer image.

Remember to remember and dare to dream

*

There are two paths weaving their way into your footballing future. There is the destructive 'never' path and there is the 'yet' path. The 'yet' path helps you become the very best you can be.

When you start to banish 'never' from your soccer speak, and you begin to take the path of 'yet', so your soccer image starts to change. It changes from a 'can't do' to a 'can do'. It changes from destructive pessimism to energising optimism. It changes from a vision of bleak to a vision of peak.

Being into mastery also helps a soccer player manage the tough times he or she may be presented with. I want all footballers to TAPP mastery. I want them to trust their ability, to accept the challenges that arise, to remain patient at all times and to focus on the process of improvement.

Learn, develop, improve…

Never say never, always say yet, and TAPP mastery.

Conclusion – Some Feedback

Hi. Come in and take a seat, I've got some exciting things to share with you.

I've been watching you at the club lately and I've seen some changes, some *big* changes.

The way you've been holding yourself. The way you've been interacting with others. It's like you think you have a bottomless pit of potential! You look wide-eyed and alive. You look so free and fearless.

That stare, that look in your eye. You train, you play, and you think like there are no limits to your ability. I love that! It sends a shiver down my spine just thinking about your enthusiasm to learn, to be the very best you can be.

The training script you gave me looks like you've put some effort into analysing your game. I like the way you know what your idea of *better* looks like. And you've formulated a plan to get there – very impressive!

Since you've constructed your script, you've been really focused. I've seen some mistakes, of course that's part of the improvement process, but the way you have been dealing with them has been great to see. I can see you really having to think about the plays in your training script. I can see you thinking, thinking, thinking. I like that. I know that you'll continue to play with improved quality as a consequence. Your brain is changing – it will take time but you will get there.

Keep reaching and keep stretching…

Then there's been those couple of games you've played. I've been impressed. You looked so in control of yourself. It looks like you've been immersed in your match script. The times things didn't go your way, you seemed to get back into position and be completely unaffected. Your body language has been superb. You look bulletproof. You look relentless!

If I was to sum up your game I would use words like confident and energetic. Your new boost of confidence has really shown on the pitch and you've delivered confident performances. You have also looked full of energy, even in the last ten minutes when everyone else has been so tired.

What else? There's definitely more…

You don't know this but I saw you take a couple of minutes of quiet time before the last match started. What were you doing? Were you picturing your script? I like that idea – I like the fact that you built the perfect process in your mind and visualised it.

And then there was your analysis after the match. I was blown away by the detail you went into. You took away the positives and the areas you wanted to improve.

I'm so impressed.

But I think I'm most impressed with you as a person. You radiate confidence. You look so optimistic. Sure, you don't get it right all the time and there have been a few disappointments, but you've stuck to your tasks positively. Your reactions and responses to setbacks have been superb. You look focused and disciplined. You look passionate. You look like you believe in yourself. You look ready for any challenge that is thrown at you…

…you look Soccer Tough.

Other Books by Dan Abrahams

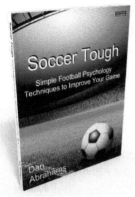

Soccer Tough: Simple Football Psychology Techniques to Improve Your Game | Dan Abrahams

"Take a minute to slip into the mind of one of the world's greatest soccer players and imagine a stadium around you. Picture a performance under the lights and mentally play the perfect game."

Technique, speed and tactical execution are crucial components of winning soccer, but it is mental toughness that marks out the very best players – the ability to play when pressure is highest, the opposition is strongest, and fear is greatest. Top players and coaches understand the importance of sport psychology in soccer but how do you actually train your mind to become the best player you can be? Soccer Tough demystifies this crucial side of the game and offers practical techniques that will enable soccer players of all abilities to actively develop focus, energy, and confidence. Soccer Tough will help banish the fear, mistakes, and mental limits that holds players back.

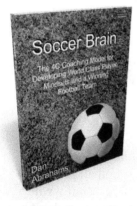

Soccer Brain: The 4C Coaching Model for Developing World Class Player Mindsets and a Winning Football Team | Dan Abrahams

The environment that a coach creates, and the relationships formed with players, is the bedrock of performance and achievement. Coaches who are able to deliver students of the game, and who are able to help players execute skills and tactics under pressure are the future leaders of the world's most loved sport. Soccer Brain teaches coaches to train players to compete with confidence, with commitment, with intelligence, and as part of a team. The positive messages from each chapter of Soccer Brain help coaches to develop players through patience, repetition, reinforcement, re-appraisal and high value relationships. Soccer Brain is for the no limits coach. It's for the coach who is passionate about developing players and building a winning team.

Other Books from Bennion Kearny

Soccer Training Blueprints: 15 Ready-to-Run Sessions for Outstanding Attacking Play
by James Jordan

Are you a busy coach and time is tight? Would you like to get hands on with ready-to-use session templates quickly? Then this book is for you! Utilising a game-based approach to soccer – where individuals actually play games rather than growing old in semi-static drills – author James Jordan offers 15 detailed session plans (comprised of 75 cutting-edge exercises) to help coaches develop attacking mindsets and improved skills in their players, and, most of all, nurture a love for soccer. Through his approach, James has won six High School State Championships and one Classic 1 Boys' Club Championship over the past decade. Aimed at coaches of both young male and female players, from 5-18 years of age, and adaptable depending on age group and skill set, each illustrated session plan is organized in an easy-to-understand format. This is the sister book to The Volunteer Soccer Coach (if you already have a copy of this book, do not purchase Soccer Training Blueprints).

The Footballer's Journey: real-world advice on becoming and remaining a professional footballer by Dean Caslake and Guy Branston

Many youngsters dream of becoming a professional footballer. But football is a highly competitive world where only a handful will succeed. Many aspiring soccer players don't know exactly what to expect, or what is required, to make the transition from the amateur world to the 'bright lights' in front of thousands of fans. The Footballer's Journey maps out the footballer's path with candid insight and no-nonsense advice. It examines the reality of becoming a footballer including the odds of 'making it', how academies really work, the importance of attitude and mindset, and even the value of having a backup plan if things don't quite work out.

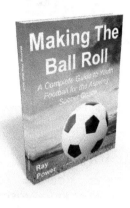

Making The Ball Roll: A Complete Guide to Youth Football for the Aspiring Soccer Coach by Ray Power

Making the Ball Roll is the ultimate complete guide to coaching youth soccer.

This focused and easy-to-understand book details training practices and tactics, and goes on to show you how to help young players achieve peak performance through tactical preparation, communication, psychology, and age-specific considerations. Each chapter covers, in detail, a separate aspect of coaching to give you, the football coach, a broad understanding of youth soccer development. Each topic is brought to life by the stories of real coaches working with real players. Never before has such a comprehensive guide to coaching soccer been found in the one place. If you are a new coach, or just trying to improve your work with players - and looking to invest in your future - this is a must-read book!

Developing the Modern Footballer through Futsal by Michael Skubala and Seth Burkett

Aimed at coaches of all levels and ages, Developing the Modern Footballer through Futsal is a concise and practical book that provides an easy-to-understand and comprehensive guide to the ways in which futsal can be used as a development tool for football. From defending and attacking to transitional play and goalkeeping, this book provides something for everyone and aims to get you up-and-running fast.

Over 50 detailed sessions are provided, with each one related to specific football scenarios and detailing how performance in these scenarios can be improved through futsal. From gegenpressing to innovative creative play under pressure, this book outlines how futsal can be used to develop a wide range of football-specific skills, giving your players the edge.

We publish a lot of books aimed at coaches, players, and football fans. Learn More about our Books at:

www.BennionKearny.com/Soccer

More Books from Bennion Kearny

Deliberate Soccer Practice: 50 Defending Football Exercises to Improve Decision-Making | Ray Power

Deliberate Soccer Practice: 50 Passing & Possession Football Exercises to Improve Decision-Making | Ray Power

Let's Talk Soccer: Using Game-Calls to Develop Communication in Football | Gérard Jones

What is Tactical Periodization? | Xavier Tamarit

Coaching Psychological Skills in Youth Football: Developing The 5Cs | Chris Harwood and Richard Anderson

The Modern Soccer Coach: Position-Specific Training | Gary Curneen

Paul Webb Academy: Strength Training for Footballers | Paul Webb

Soccer Tactics 2014: What the World Cup Taught Us | Ray Power

Universality - The Blueprint for Soccer's New Era: How Germany and Pep Guardiola Are Showing Us the Future Football Game | Matthew Whitehouse

The Modern Soccer Coach 2014: A Four Dimensional Approach | Gary Curneen

Scientific Approaches to Goalkeeping in Football: A Practical Perspective on the Most Unique Position in Sport | Andy Elleray

The Bundesliga Blueprint: How Germany became the Home of Football | Lee Price

Printed in the USA
CPSIA information can be obtained
at www.ICGtesting.com
CBHW071215130524
8479CB00011B/452